SIMPLE QUILTS

...ke a Million Bucks

Nicole C. Chambers

quilt ma•ni•ac (kwilt máyneeak) *n.*
A person who loves quilting with
unbridled exuberance and zest.

TIGER LILY PRESS

To Justin

An extraordinary soul

Acknowledgments

A heartfelt thank you to —

The Parker family, for allowing me to invade their elegant showroom and use their beautiful furniture to photograph the quilts for this book. A very special thank you to Cheryl Parker who made it all possible.

Pat Chittenden, whose kind heart and generosity never ceases to amaze me. How lucky I am to count you as my friend.

Chris Murrell, for being a most excellent photo stylist and giving me the benefit of your fabulous talent for creating visual delights.

Jan Bechler, Julie Kastl, Carol Ann Langstine, Marian Scott & Berniece Skinner, for volunteering to be my guinea pigs and helping to test the instructions. What fun you all are.

All of my friends, who offered their best advice when asked and never admitted to being tired of hearing "how the book was coming along."

And especially to Aaron, who is always in my corner through sunshine and rain. You delight my heart.

Editor: Aaron Chambers
Photography: Nick Garibbo
              Photo Design

Photo Stylist: Chris Murrell
              Seams Sew Right Quilt Shop

*The gorgeous furniture and accessories
you see in the photographs can be found at*
Parker Furniture
10375 SW Beaverton-Hills Highway
Beaverton, Oregon 97005
(503) 644-0155
www.parker-furniture.com

Published by:

Tiger Lily Press
PO Box 740
Depoe Bay, Oregon 97341
(541) 764-2778
www.quiltmaniac.com

Publisher's Cataloging-in-Publication Data

Chambers, Nicole C.
    Simple quilts that look like a million bucks / Nicole C. Chambers. – 1st ed.
    p. cm.
    Includes index.
    LCCN: 2002094709
    ISBN: 0-9708375-2-6

    1. Patchwork quilts. 2. Patchwork–Patterns.
    3. Color in textile crafts. I. Title.

TT835.C43 2004   746.46

Every effort has been made to insure that the contents of this publication are as accurate and correct as possible. The author and publisher cannot be responsible for human error, typographical mistakes or variations in individual work. Neither author nor publisher assumes any responsibility for any injuries suffered or for damages or other loss incurred that result from the material herein. All instructions and diagrams should be carefully reviewed and clearly understood before beginning any project.

Printed in China
10 9 8 7 6 5 4 3 2 1

Contents

Longarm Quilter Extraordinaire

Merline McLaughlin
The Cotton Yard
Eugene, Oregon
(541) 689-5128
cottonyard@juno.com

I am often amazed by how much personality and dimension excellent quilting contributes to the overall charisma of a quilt. Whether you decorate your wall with the quilt, toss it over a bed or use it to wrap up the baby, it's the quilting that adds that final touch of texture and mystique. Perhaps that is why quilts have earned the reputation of being both objects of art and affection.

Although Merline McLaughlin and I started out working together as virtual strangers, we have become good friends through the course of this project. It's been particularly fun and rewarding for me to have practically unlimited creative freedom to propose quilting ideas. In our collaboration of the quilting designs within the pages of this book, Merline not only contributed many excellent ideas, she then used her skill and mastery of quilting to turn these ideas into the impressive examples of longarm quilting that you see. I particularly love her "take no prisoners" attitude. With the multitude of ideas we tossed around, some realistic ... some not, never once did she say something could not be done. Instead, she directed her energies towards making it happen. To my way of thinking, it's this attribute that sets the artisan apart from the technician.

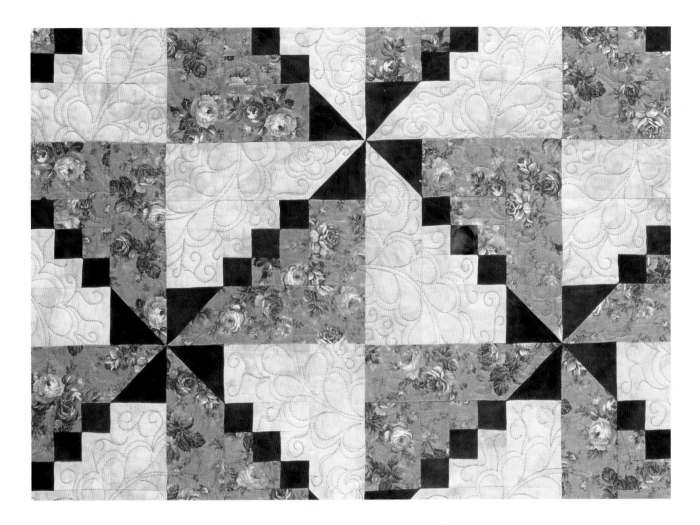

Working as a professional longarm quilter for some years, Merline specializes in providing high quality quilting to her clientele. Although known for her meticulously executed custom quilting *(such as the quilted paisley pattern you see on page 18 in this book)* she also has a very special technique of doing "custom allover" quilting. This technique is an outstanding combination of freehand custom quilting with an allover quilting philosophy. Used well, it is a fabulous and practical way to add beauty and texture to many quilts. When Merline is not quilting, she spends her time teaching those special techniques to other longarm quilters, whether they are beginners learning the ropes or experienced professionals wanting to update their skills.

It is my hope that you enjoy taking a close look at the quilting details of the quilts within this book, and let them inspire you. They serve as a shining example of Merline's creativity and skill, transforming what started out as musings and doodles and turning them into fabulously textured quilts. ■

Turning Problem Fabrics Into Treasures

One of the fastest … easiest … and most overlooked secrets to creating delightful and charming quilts is to make good use of directional and geometric fabrics. As you can see from the designs in this book, stripes and polka dots are my particular favorites from this group. If these types of prints are not your cup of tea, please note that there are many less obvious directional or geometric fabrics that will perform beautifully as well.

Quite unfairly, these visually strong fabrics have gotten much maligned as being hard to work with.

Although not true, this reputation persists. Since cutting these prints off kilter can often be so easily spotted, many quilters consider that proof positive, and avoid using them like the plague. This is unfortunate. It is true that to use these fabrics effectively some extra attention is required, but it is really more a matter of learning a few simple tricks in handling these fabrics.

Believe it or not, for many quilters, the trouble starts when they cut a directional fabric without taking notice that it is directional. In some instances, such as in the case of stripes, it is of course obvious. But in the heat of the "creative moment" the print dynamics of many subtler directionals can go unnoticed. Not until the pieces are cut up and sewn together is it realized that the print is going every which way, giving a visually unsettling result.

The second objection many quilters have is that they like directional fabrics to be cut so they look straight. It must be confessed that I'm a member of this club as well. Although we can appreciate the charm of the topsy turvy look in many quilts, it is important to us that the fabrics in our quilts are cut so they look straight. Most of the time, this is quite easily accomplished by just following a few easy steps.

First and foremost, before buying any directional or geometrically spaced fabric *(such as classic polka dots or checks)* check how straight the print is on the fabric. Sometimes, a print can be printed just fine but will get pulled out of shape when it is rolled onto the bolt. If that's the case, it's usually not worth trying to pull the fabric back into shape. If you find that the print is fairly straight on the lengthwise grain but leaning a little here or there across the width, it will still more than likely work. Some prints, however, are quite literally beyond salvage. So if you don't want to use them leaning this way and that, it may be best to pass them by.

The simple trick to cutting directional fabrics is, instead of cutting across the fabric as you normally would, you cut your strips from the length of the fabric. The reason for this is that when fabric is woven, the threads that run the length of the fabric have almost no give while the threads running across the width of the fabric have quite a bit. Take a scrap square of fabric and try it out for yourself. You'll notice that there is quite a bit of stretch in one direction and hardly any in the other. Because of this fact, when fabric is printed, the print almost always runs straighter up and down the fabric rather than across. To make our pieces look straight, we are going to use this fact to our advantage, and cut the strips in concert with the straightest part of the print. By the way, if you are making the patterns in this book, the instructions are already geared to these special cutting techniques. Follow the outlined steps when the sample quilt isn't showing a striped fabric.

To begin, cut a 21" section from the length of your yardage. Although it's slightly more work, you will get a much better result if from this point forward you cut the strips from a single layer of fabric. Turn the fabric so that you are now cutting your strips across the 21" edge of the fabric. *(Note that your strips will be 21" in length, which is half of a typical strip so you may need to make the appropriate adjustments for that fact in your cutting instructions.)*

Trim off the selvage and give yourself a straight edge to cut the strips from by lining up your ruler against one of the stripes *(or a row of motifs if you are using polka dots or another geometric or directional fabric)*. Cut your strips as you normally would from this edge, occasionally resquaring your fabric so that your strips are cutting straight with the print. Sub-cut or strip piece your strips as you normally would.

In some instances, you will need to rethink your strip widths before cutting to be sure your stripes are running in the direction you intend. This is particularly important if your directions are for a quilt that does not show a striped fabric.

In instances where the geometric print is pulled slightly out of shape across the width of the fabric, you'll notice that the print may lean a little when you sub-cut. If this happens don't worry; they will still more than likely look straight in your quilt. Often times, since the larger area of the fabric is running straight, the eye doesn't notice the smaller areas that are slightly askew.

The next time you see fabrics you previously thought were too hard to work with … indulge yourself. Cool and nifty stripes truly are an instant way of adding real zip and style to many quilt designs. Don't limit yourself; collect all types, from the traditional to the funky, even fabrics that aren't striped per se but just have a vertical feel to them will add an interesting dimension to your quilt.

As you become familiar in handling these fabrics you will find more and more uses for them. The strong linear design elements of directional fabrics will add interest and drama to most quilt designs. You can create all types of optical illusions almost instantly. For example, take a look at *Feel the Vibe.* The wavy stripes add so much motion and energy that the quilt, quite literally, almost vibrates with energy. Even when cut into the very basic shape of a square, the fabric gives this quilt personality and energy, with no extra

effort from you. By contrast, in *Cambridge Rose* the stripes form a soft chevron design, adding a touch of sophistication while at the same time remaining light and charming. The classic taupe stripe in *Victoria Garden* make the block visually radiate from the center creating interest and understated elegance.

You can even use these types of fabric to create a graphical contrast, giving yourself more latitude with color options when making a quilt using very soft colors. In *Sweet Dreams,* the classic stripe helps to showcase the pinwheel design without making it necessary to use strong or highly contrasting colors, allowing the soft look to remain intact. The use of the wavy stripe in the small pinwheels adds a bit of fun while keeping the quilt from being overwhelmed with stripes. Directional fabrics can be real style makers. ■

Let the Quilting be the Star

The process of choosing fabric prints and colors for a quilt can become such an all consuming event that the concept of letting the fabrics play second fiddle to the quilting doesn't readily even occur to us. How easy it is to overlook an absolutely stellar opportunity to make a quilt a real show stopper. Besides, by letting the fabric become the quilting canvas, so to speak, we can produce a fabulous quilt while having made only the simplest of fabric choices.

Whether you intend to make the quilting the focal point of your quilt or not, it will serve your interests very very well if you give some thought as to how you may want the quilt quilted while you are in the process of choosing fabrics. But if you are like most of us, only when the quilt top is finished will you start wondering how best to quilt it. If no ideas come readily to mind, the obvious answer may seem to ask your favorite longarm quilter what they think will look good on it.

Although almost all longarm quilters relish the idea of being part of the creative design process, it's unfair to transfer our "zero design idea" burden onto their shoulders without even some concepts and suggestions to start the ball rolling.

Secondly, you are giving up a stupendously, great, fabulous way to create all sorts of special effects on your quilt. Quite certainly, you don't need me to tell you that how a quilt top is quilted has a huge effect on its final look. Sometimes, you can even solve design problems that weren't realized until the quilt top was finished. For instance, if a fabric ends up looking too light, too dark or just too bright, you can tone things down or brighten them up through the choice of thread and quilting style.

Spending time thinking about quilting thread color in general will pay off handsomely as well. Thread color can make or break how even excellent quilting looks, and of course it has a strong impact on the finished effect of the quilt. It can actually give the quilt a whole new personality.

Deciding on your quilting before making the quilt can even completely revolutionize the fabrics you end up using. Case in point is *Lynley Manor*. Believe it or not, this quilt started life in bubblegum pink, banana yellow and black. Screams retro to the max doesn't it? On a lark, I showed a test block to Merline *(my long-*

arm quilter) at one of our meetings, and we ended up kicking around some quilting ideas. Both of us agreed that paisley quilting would be big retro fun. On our next meeting, Merline surprised me with a drawing of the paisley pattern that our conversation had inspired. Two things happened. One, I fell in love. Two, I made the immediate decision that there was no way the pink, yellow and black fabrics would show off this fabulous paisley pattern to its best advantage. Choosing the color scheme that became *Lynley Manor* turned into

a complete no brainer. Visualizing the quilting in a rich golden thread made choosing the quilt fabrics of black, burgundy and gold a complete cinch. The result, as you see, is a quilt that looks luxuriously old world, rich and elegant – and only 3 fairly ordinary fabrics were used in a very simple block design. *(By the way, if you too love the quilted paisley design, you can have it quilted on your quilt as well. Merline has added it to her quilting repertoire.)* ◼

Gray: The Undeserving Wallflower

The problem with gray fabric is that unless you really like gray or have already found out the marvelous addition gray makes to many quilts, it just seems to sit on the shelf without much notice from anyone.

If there is ever an award given to the most undeserving fabric wallflower, gray will get it hands down. After all, it's pretty easy to skip past "the gray section" in a quilt shop when there are so many other spunky colors vying for our attention. And although some quilters have fairly strong opinions on certain colors — the most common response to seeing gray used in a quilt is that it never occurred to them as a viable color consideration. Imagine all the gray fabrics crying themselves to sleep over that one. They, after all, have much to offer your quilt.

A judicious addition of gray can make many color schemes a little more interesting, adding an air of sophistication almost instantly. Grays can add softness in a most subtle way as well. It is a great addition when you want to mellow bold colors; the colors are still perceived as vibrant, but now they'll be using their indoor voice. In an already soft color scheme, gray can add a touch of elegance. For instance, you could easily imagine a quilt made of soft yellow and white looking feminine and airy. Add gray to the mix, and although your color palette remains soft, it now sports an urbane chic feel.

Although all grays often get slotted as neutrals without too much thought, there are actually many variances of gray. It's important to pay attention to the undertones of the grays you are considering. A true neutral gray won't have any cool or warm undertones and will therefore work well in most color circumstances. Many gray fabrics, however, have a definite cool or warm undertone. You'll notice that warm grays have a yellowish, almost mauve or taupe cast, while cool grays lean towards blue, purple and sometimes even have a greenish cast.

Based on how you are using it, the warmth or coolness of the gray will have an impact on the effect you are creating. If in the past you have tried using grays and it just didn't work for you, it's quite likely the problem may have been that the color temperature was not quite right or the value was too light or dark in regards to the other surrounding fabrics.

Do yourself a favor. The next time you're in a quilt shop, swing by the gray section and bring an appealing one home to your stash … even if in the moment the purple fabric seems like a lot more fun. ∎

Creating Color Pizzazz

All too often, quilters spend much time and energy painstakingly searching for just the perfect matches to their focus fabric. Then, when the quilt is finished, they find themselves wondering what is missing … after all they worked so hard to get the colors just right.

Taking a focus fabric and closely matching coordinating colors to it will only give you a certain kind of quilt. If you want your quilt to "look like a million bucks" you have to be willing to take a few color risks.

When visiting quilt shops, it is sometimes particularly fun for me to help quilters pick out fabrics for their next quilt *(incognito, so to speak)*. So if lately you've been helped by a stranger showing you things you thought a little odd, *(just think)* it could have been me. Although to date everyone I've assisted has been kind and polite, more than one face reflected the thought "what ARE you thinking" at some of my suggestions.

If you aren't completely familiar with the pliability of color, it's an understandable reaction. It is important to always remember that color is never constant. As colors move in and out of the company of other colors, they never stay the same. If colors had a zodiac sign, you can bet it would be Gemini. The good news is this gives much leeway in

adding colors to your quilt which are different from those in your focus fabric. The magical part is that you can get them to look as though they were made for each other.

It would not be a surprise if you gave me that "what are you thinking" look after all *Samurai Garden's* fabrics were laid in front of you while still on the bolt. This quilt is an interesting mix of fabric

colors and motifs. As you can see, the focus fabric is predominantly black with soft pink and vivid red flowers, as well as some tan, orange and light green accents. In the quilt, these fabric pieces are then surrounded by fabric that is predominantly gray with black, dark orange and very light peach accents. This fabric combination is then accented with a fairly strong pink that matches none of the pinks within the prints but is within their color family in terms

of color saturation and temperature. The taupe and black print could have been a risky choice if the print's personality was not so in-sync with the theme of the quilt and the black and taupe weren't evenly balanced within the print itself. The little bits of tan in the focus fabric also helped in creating an overall color harmony as well.

Although the colors are not a match, they start looking as though they are. Chances are, if the individual color details hadn't been pointed out, you wouldn't have actively even thought about them. You can create wonderful color illusions by experimenting and adding colors that are not the exact colors you see in your focus fabric, giving you a lot of freedom for making fabric choices with pizzazz.

When choosing fabrics, it's important to keep in mind that your goal is to find fabrics that will work in unity rather than fabrics that match. These colors are free to maintain their individuality, while still working together in a cohesive way.

If you find you have a strong tendency to want to match things, don't beat yourself up over it. The truth is, we all fall into the matching mindset at one time or another. When you are working on your next quilt and find it's lacking that

little spark, give yourself a quick check and see if the matching bug has been at work.

Sometimes what will really spark a quilt is adding colors that aren't even mentioned in the focus fabric. Doing that, however, can really work up that little voice inside of your head — so be ready to tell it "sit down and be quiet" when it energetically points out that the fabrics you are using don't match at all!

Adding new colors to the focus fabric color scheme, when making *Indian Summer,* was actually very easy to do. In this instance, they simply finished the concept the focus fabric started. As you can see, the focus fabric is an obvious autumn motif. It contains several golds, a rust or two, olive green and a dark red on a black background. Maintaining the quilt color scheme to only those fabrics would have severely limited the visual impact of this quilt. Adding the purples, burgundy, tan, orange and lime green was really not even much of a risk. Since they are all familiar autumn colors, they simply added to the mood of the focus fabric. Just because they were not included in the focus fabric palette did not mean the quilt would not benefit from having them.

An important trick to creating color illusions is to view all your

fabrics at a distance of at least 6 feet. Do that in the quilt shop before buying them; do that in your sewing room when deciding who's in or out; do that while you are making the quilt. What you see at 6 feet is a much more accurate picture of the color's interaction than what you see at arm's length.

Although we've discussed color at length in *The Quilt Maniac's Playbook,* a small

refresher here may be helpful. What you need to keep in mind when it comes to color is that color is never constant. It is constantly changing and how it changes depends on what color or group of colors you place next to each other. Keeping this fact in mind will be a HUGE help when you are putting colors together for your next quilt. That is how the fabrics in *Samurai Garden* make a harmo-

nious statement, even though they have some significant differences individually.

All colors will work together if you get the value, saturation, and temperature combination in a good balance. As you know, value is the lightness or the darkness of a color. We often call these graduations shades. When you say "this shade of violet is very light" it also means that the value of the violet is very high. What value a color is, is also completely relative to what surrounds it. A medium blue placed next to a light yellow will be perceived as the dark value, while the same blue placed next to navy will become the light value.

Color saturation or color intensity on the other hand, simply refers to the vividness or dullness of a color. Colors that have been softened or dulled by a gray overcast, such as steel blue or sage green, are of low intensity and saturation. How light or dark a color is, is NOT affected by the intensity of that color. Color saturation or intensity refers only to the clearness *(absence of gray)* or dullness *(presence of gray)* of a color.

When it comes to color temperature, each color family has been assigned to belong to either a warm or cool temperature group. The reds, oranges and yellows and all their various shades belong to the warm temperature group while the: blues, greens and violets belong to the cool group. Even though color families belong to one of these temperature groups, each individual shade, no matter what group their family officially belongs to, will have its own warm or cool undertone. As you work with fabrics, spend a few seconds considering whether they have a warm or cool undertone. In many instances adjusting the warmth or coolness of a color is all that is needed to make colors work well together. ■

How to Create a Color Scheme
Without Using a Focus Fabric

a little going a long way. Used only in the pinwheels and chain, the eggplant purple defines the quilt's design and gives the quilt presence, while the remaining 2 fabrics keep the quilt's overall appearance delicate.

There are times when you can be more liberal in your use of the dark accent fabric without disturbing the soft look of the quilt. For instance, the dark floral fabric in *Jasmine* is used quite generously by comparison. Yet, it still successfully maintains a soft look even though this fabric has a black background. Notice the flower motif within the print is large and

is printed in muted colors. This helps not only to maintain the soft personality of the quilt, but also helps to diffuse the severity that a larger amount of black would introduce to this color scheme. A fabric showing a larger proportion of black would have been too heavy handed. Again, it is proportion that plays the dominant role. The soft colors within this quilt easily outnumber the dark floral 4 to 1. The next time you try your hand at this type of color scheme … remember the secret is balance and proportion. ■

Vertical Quilts: An Easy Way to Make a Big Statement

For reasons that remain a mystery, many quilters overlook the dramatic design potential offered by vertical quilts. Chic and elegant in florals; dramatic and vivacious in stronger fabric personalities, this type of quilt design truly offers a shortcut to making impressive quilts. Perhaps one reason quilters shy away from making vertical quilts is the lack of a clear indication of where a block starts and stops, giving the mistaken impression they are "hard to make." Ironically, in many instances a well designed vertical quilt is actually easier and faster to put together, having less piecing than many conventional block-by-block quilt designs.

Vertical quilts, by definition have a strong linear presence that carries an impressive design wallop, whether you make the quilt bed size or settle on something small and casual. Since they also lend themselves to a wide variety of quilt personalities, it's a great design choice for the favorite man in your life. By the same token, don't think they are limited to only making a vivid statement, this type of quilt will also look perfectly yummy in soft gentle tones and prints.

Aside from the multitude of interesting fabric possibilities you can concoct for the pieced areas of a vertical quilt, the real design bonus is the generously wide sashing areas. A whole new design dimension can be added to the quilt by making good use of just that space.

In making other styles of quilts, it may be your experience that, generally speaking, it is important to keep the sashing fabric on the subtler, quieter side. Vertical quilts, on the other hand, work quite well when the sashing fabric is left to steal the show, or at least hog a fair amount of the limelight. Many times you can create absolutely wonderful and interesting effects by playing the sashing area to the hilt. Just remember, you want to preserve a good balance of interest between the pieced section and the sashing treatment you decide on. Letting the sashing help carry the design responsibility is a wonderful design tool and you don't even have to piece to reap the benefits!

35

As we explore the design possibilities vertical quilts offer, you may be delighted to realize that this sashing area is a tremendous place to show off those beautiful linear styled border prints. Many exquisite florals have been printed in this fabric style. Quite certainly you've even admired them and wondered along with the rest of us, what you could ever do with them. Since these fabrics need to be used in a solid length to realize the print's potential, many of these fabrics are lying about unused in our stash. Great news! You can use these types of prints easily and with abandon in your next vertical quilt.

You can also make great use of the sashing area to showcase a favorite fabric without defusing its wonderful print by cutting it into small bits. Nor do you need to push it into the responsibility of becoming the focus fabric. Generally we think of the focus fabric as … well … being the star of the show. Notice how in the case of *Fishing Rock Lodge,* the only printed fabric within the quilt is the beautiful batik seen in the sashing. If this fabric was used as the main focus fabric in the traditional sense, the end result would have likely been a darker, less lively quilt. Cutting up the focus fabric into smaller pieces would have also changed the entire personality of the quilt. In this case, the sashing fabric sets the unmistakable personality for the whole quilt, showing itself beautifully, while letting the other brighter and livelier fabrics have their day in the sun.

But you don't have to limit yourself to just showing off fabric prints in the sashing area. It is the perfect place to showcase quilting in a way not possible in other quilt styles. Again, the long uninterrupted area provides a very good opportunity to show quilting in a particularly dramatic way. As you may have already noticed, in *Remember Aruba* the black fabric used in the sashing is also used in the sides within the pieced sections. Aside from creating a whole new look by this dramatic use of solid black, it provides the perfect place to showcase exquisite quilting. Using gray thread gives the quilting a subtle elegance while making it even more striking.

What fabrics would you use in a vertical quilt? How would you approach working with the sashing areas? Let your creativity shine and try at least one vertical quilt but don't be surprised if you can't stop at just making one. But don't worry … we'll make more designs! ■

Don't Let Bold Colors Make You Cluck

It's easy to get the willies *(and turn chicken)* when considering a bold vibrant color for the largest area of the quilt, namely the background. It is a lot like riding on a big roller coaster. On the one hand, it's very exciting and big fun; on the other hand, it can scare the bajeebers out of you!

So not surprisingly you might find yourself at an impasse. While you know you absolutely love the color, and can just imagine how vivacious it will make your quilt look, you may also find yourself worrying that the finished quilt may blast poor Freddie out of his room. Even if you find it hard to picture how the finished quilt will actually look, don't be afraid to take the plunge and use that splashy background color. There are a few things you can do to set yourself up for success.

Although there are exceptions to every rule when it comes to quilting, consider choosing the bright background fabric from the cool color family. Using bold colors in large quantities from this group is usually a much safer choice than using warm ones. For instance, the turquoise *(a member of the blue family)* in *Calypso* is supported and accessorized by fabrics that are from the warm color group with a few tossed in from the cool family for good measure. For a moment, imagine reversing the warm/cool color ratios and using the yellow fabric, or even the fuchsia or orange for the background. Yikes! … quite an eyeful isn't it? Cool colors, even when vibrant do not become over stimulating as quickly as those from the warm group.

Even though the turquoise is quite bright in its own right, because it's from the cool family, it works as an effective canvas for showing off the other colors. And just to make sure your quilt doesn't end up becoming outlawed for being an illegal stimulant, it is important to include some calming fabrics into your color scheme. Neutral colors such as black, white, cream, tan, taupe and gray can all help tone things down. In *Calypso*, the theme fabric with all its bright tropical fish may not readily look like a calming influence but the black background along with some of the white in the print work as an effective neutralizer on this color scheme. Notice that it is also the only fabric that has a fairly busy print. Using a solid black fabric would have done the job in terms of calming the color scheme, but it would have changed the personality of the quilt completely. Aside from the theme fabric, the other fabrics have very subtle prints. It's a good rule of thumb that if you are giving the eye a lot to look at in one area *(such as color)* it's a good idea to tone down in another.

To maintain visual balance, you will want to make sure your supporting fabrics are strong and bold in their own right. Colors that are not visually strong enough to hold their own will throw the color balance out of kilter and make the background fabric look like an overdyed bully. Working with splashy colors is exciting and fun. Get yourself a sponge and a towel if you think you'll need them and roll out your bright and beautiful fabrics! ■

Quilt Gallery

From My Heart to Yours ...

The Morning Star brings sheer delight

Of vivid colors and spirits bright —

But as the day folds into velvet night

And we peer carefully at the twinkling lights —

We see our wishes reaching stars

Who will take them past Jupiter and Mars

To the Universe where all things are possible.

It is my wish that this book brings you joy, that it speaks to your creativity, filling you with that delicious energy that literally propels you into your sewing room, That the design and fabric ideas inspire you to challenge yourself in a new way ... be it wandering outside of your quilting comfort zone or something as mundane as being willing to believe that a quilt really is simple to make even if at first glance it doesn't look it. But most of all, it is my wish that when your quilt is done, you are filled with that complete satisfaction that the Cheshire cat grin was designed for.

Nicole Chambers
a self confessed quilt maniac

Morning Star

Approximate size: 85" x 108"
Made by: Nicole Chambers
Quilted by: Merline McLaughlin

Combine a simple block with some pieced sashing; add an interesting combination of colors to the mix and you have a perfect recipe of how a very simple block can become a quilt that "looks like a million bucks." This queen size quilt is long enough to go around the pillows. Instructions on page 84.

Mysteries of the Night
Approximate size: 81" x 81"
Made by: Nicole Chambers
Quilted by: Merline McLaughlin

If you looked at this quilt and thought "I love it – but it looks too involved and time consuming" ... you, my friend, are happily mistaken! This quilt is comprised of a simple block put together with pieced sashing. It's actually the sashing that creates the wonderful stars. Do yourself a favor and check out the instructions on page 92.

Alternating Currents

Approximate size: 68" x 76"
Made by: Pat Chittenden
Quilted by: Merline McLaughlin

You can create many interesting and dynamic color effects with this quilt design. Shown here, the colors are strong, bright and contrasting, making a bold statement. But imagine this quilt in pastels gently flowing into one another — gives this quilt a whole new look doesn't it? The possibilities are endless. Instructions on page 79.

Samurai Garden

Approximate size: 64" x 72"
Made by: Nicole Chambers
Quilted by: Merline McLaughlin

Depending on the fabrics you choose, this fast and simple quilt can easily take on many different personalities. Shown here with an oriental flair, notice how some of the fabrics completely blend into one another creating the quilt's mystique. This design, however, could just as easily work with fun brights or contemporary florals. Instructions on page 75.

An Amish Hound

Approximate size: 52" x 64"
Made by: Nicole Chambers
Quilted by: Merline McLaughlin

This quilt block pattern is reminiscent of hounds-tooth checks. Combining bright bold colors with gray gives this quilt an air of sophistication while the black background adds wonderful contrast, reminding one of Amish quilts — but with a bit of whimsey. The pieced border is both easy to make and a very effective finish for this quilt. Instructions on page 133.

Happy Days

Approximate size: 52" x 64"
Made by: Nicole Chambers
Quilted by: Merline McLaughlin

For reasons that are not readily apparent, this quilt block is really quite a lot of fun to make! Perhaps because it is so incredibly simple. Shown here in fabrics with a French country cottage flavor, you can't help but be reminded of fruit, cheese, and crusty bread. This is a great choice for a first quilt or when you want something really fast and easy. Instructions on page 133.

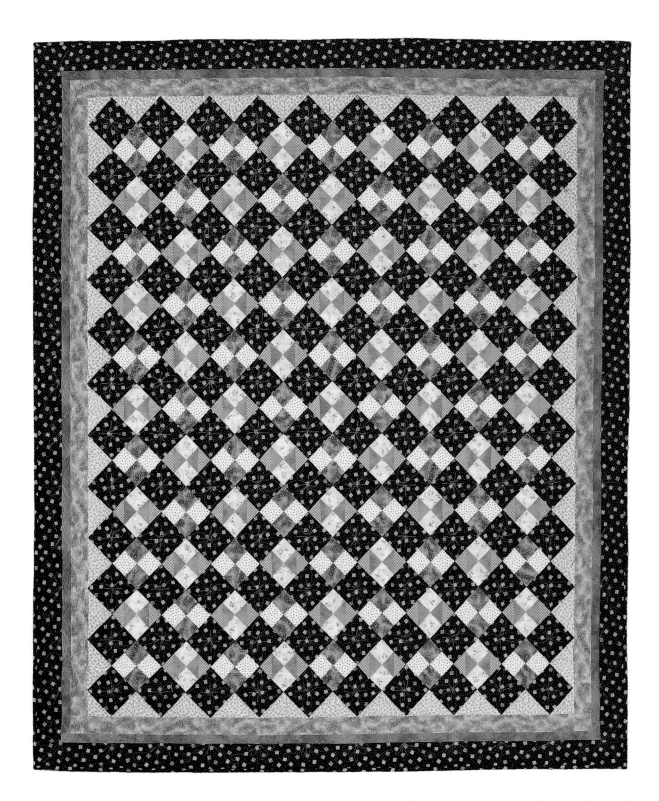

Sassy Girl

Approximate size: 68" x 80"
Made by: Nicole Chambers
Quilted by: Merline McLaughlin

Have you ever wanted to put colors together that ... well ... aren't usually thought of as going together? The next time you are feeling a little sassy yourself, make your version of this quilt. It goes together so easily that it won't even feel dangerous to be a little experimental. Instructions on page 71.

Feel the Vibe

Approximate size: 68" x 80"
Made by: Nicole Chambers
Quilted by: Merline McLaughlin

If you've ever fallen in love with a zany striped fabric, such as the focus fabric in this quilt, and wondered what in the world you could ever do with it. Good news! This quilt is the perfect place to show it off, giving your quilt both style and personality with no extra effort. Instructions on page 71.

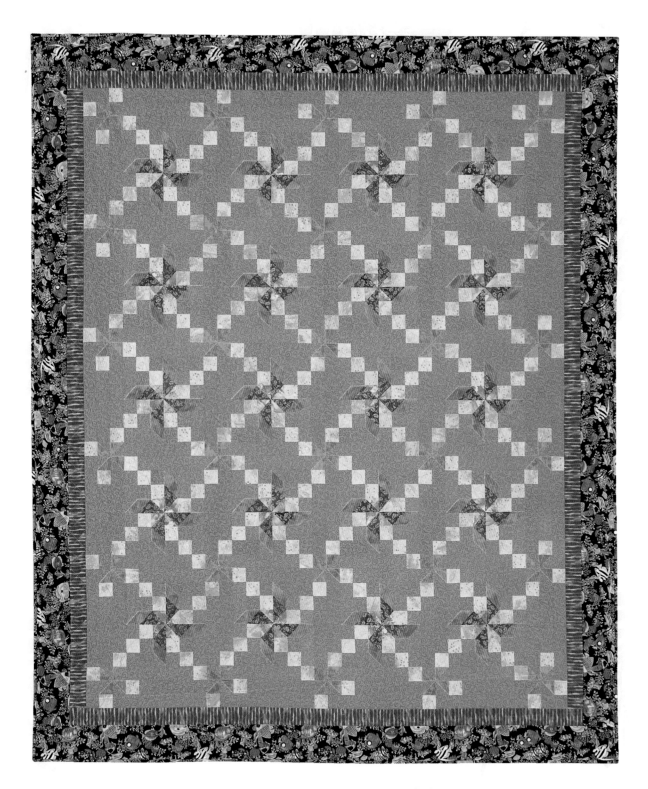

Calypso

Approximate size: 87" x 104"
Made by: Nicole Chambers
Quilted by: Merline McLaughlin

Inspired by the bright colorful beauty of tropical fish swimming in a crystal clear ocean, this quilt makes a wonderfully bright and happy color statement. Don't shy away from using strong background colors, the bright turquoise is what gives this quilt its pizzazz. Instructions on page 106.

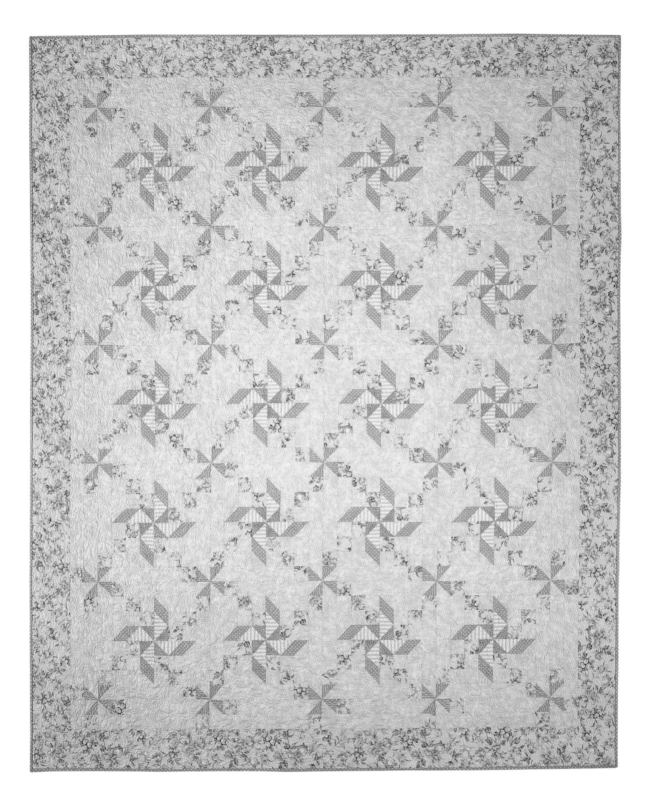

Sweet Dreams

Approximate size: 84" x 98"
Made by: Nicole Chambers
Quilted by: Merline McLaughlin

Pinwheels ... stripes ... dots ... florals — you can hardly go wrong with that combination. Create a wonderfully soft and comforting quilt by using fabrics with contrasting motifs rather than strong contrasts of color value. Instructions on page 106.

Cambridge Rose

Approximate size: 67" x 77"
Made by: Nicole Chambers
Quilted by: Merline McLaughlin

Unfortunately many quilters shy away from using stripes, mistakenly thinking that they are difficult to use. This pattern gives you easy step-by-step instructions so your stripes will form the subtle chevron design without a lot of fuss. It's a simple yet fabulous way to add an interesting design dimension to this soft floral quilt. Instructions on page 117.

Indian Summer

Approximate size: 65" x 78"
Made by: Nicole Chambers
Quilted by: Merline McLaughlin

Some quilts simply beg to have many different fabrics in them. The lush colors of autumn leaves you see here are particularly easy to work with. But don't be afraid to be a little daring and mix in a few brights. If scrappy quilts are hard for you, this is an easy quilt to experiment with. Instructions on page 113.

Remember Aruba

Approximate size: 67" x 77"
Made by: Nicole Chambers
Quilted by: Merline McLaughlin

This vertical quilt comes together surprisingly fast. Dramatic in its own right by the strong linear design, the black sashing adds a wonderful contrast to the rich colors of the batiks. It also provides a fabulous opportunity to showcase your quilting. Instructions on page 100.

Fishing Rock Lodge

Approximate size: 75" x 86"
Made by: Pat Chittenden
Quilted by: Merline McLaughlin

The focus fabric doesn't always have to end up being the main focus. Used generously in the sashing and border, it gives this quilt a strong personality while the rich colors of the supporting fabrics actually steal the show. Instructions on page 100.

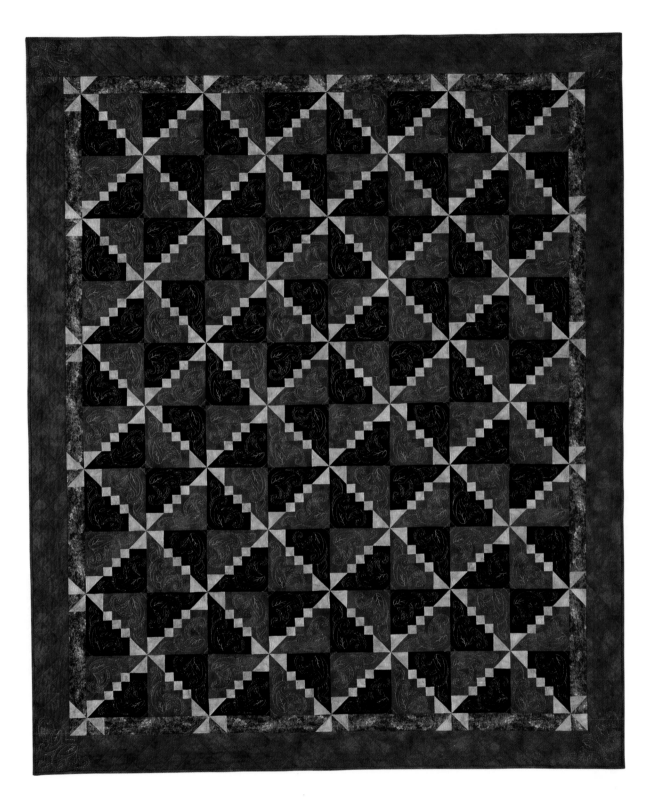

Lynley Manor

Approximate size: 85" x 102"
Made by: Nicole Chambers
Quilted by: Merline McLaughlin

Rich in elegance and old world charm, this quilt is the perfect place to showcase beautiful quilting. If you've fallen hopelessly in love with the luxurious paisley quilting design pictured on this quilt — don't despair, Merline has added this fabulous design to her regular quilting repertoire. Instructions on page 66.

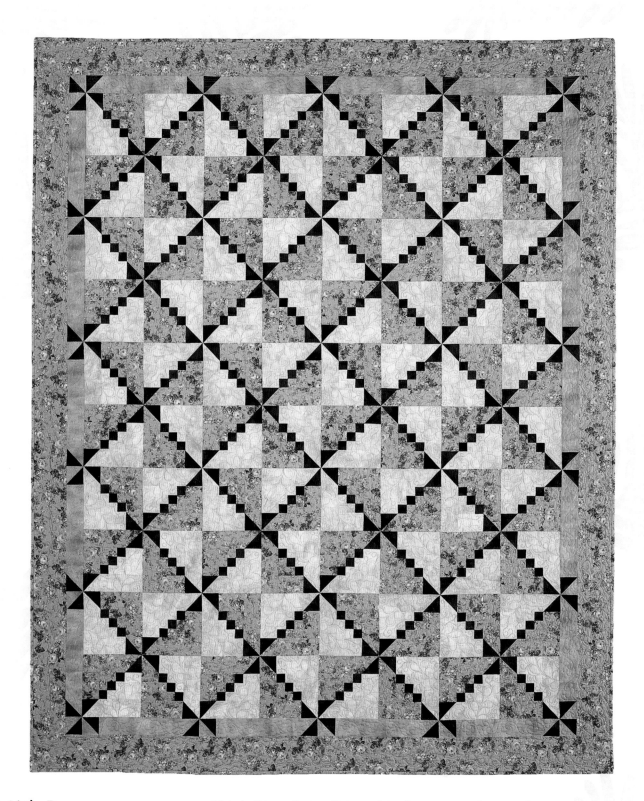

A Little Romance

Approximate size: 85" x 102"
Made by: Pat Chittenden
Quilted by: Merline McLaughlin

This is the perfect quilt to make when you need a stunning queen size quilt but find yourself short on time. Made from a very simple block, this quilt design lends itself beautifully to a multitude of color combinations. A great choice when you need a quick wedding gift. Instructions on page 66.

Vivaldi

Approximate size: 76" x 76"
Made by: Nicole Chambers
Quilted by: Merline McLaughlin

To the uninitiated eye, this quilt could mislead you into thinking that it's ... well ... hard to make. Don't you be fooled! When putting the rows together, you will have to match the seams, but aside from that the unique construction techniques makes sewing this quilt a simple proposition. Instructions on page 122.

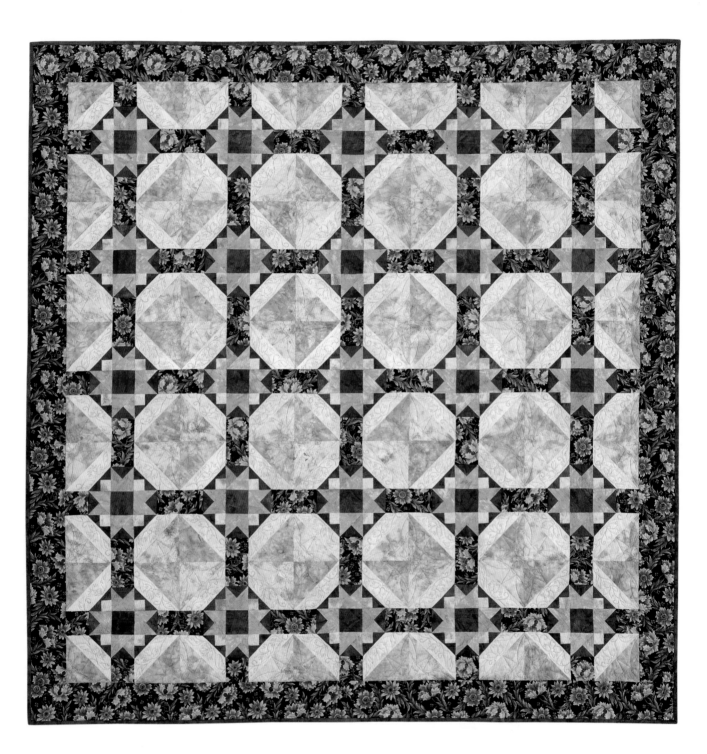

Jasmine

Approximate size: 76" x 76"
Made by: Nicole Chambers
Quilted by: Merline McLaughlin

The mix of soft delicious colors make this quilt look almost good enough to eat. Don't shy away from combining soft colors with a dramatic dark print. In good proportions this combination can go far in making a soft yet striking quilt. Instructions on page 122.

Victoria Garden

Approximate size: 68" x 68"
Made by: Nicole Chambers
Quilted by: Merline McLaughlin

The combination of dots and stripes in this quilt turn a simple block into an elegant affair. The antique quality of the floral along with the use of black and pink give this quilt a decidedly Victorian feel, but you could just as easily give it a contemporary garden or country cottage look by merely changing the colors. Instructions on page 128.

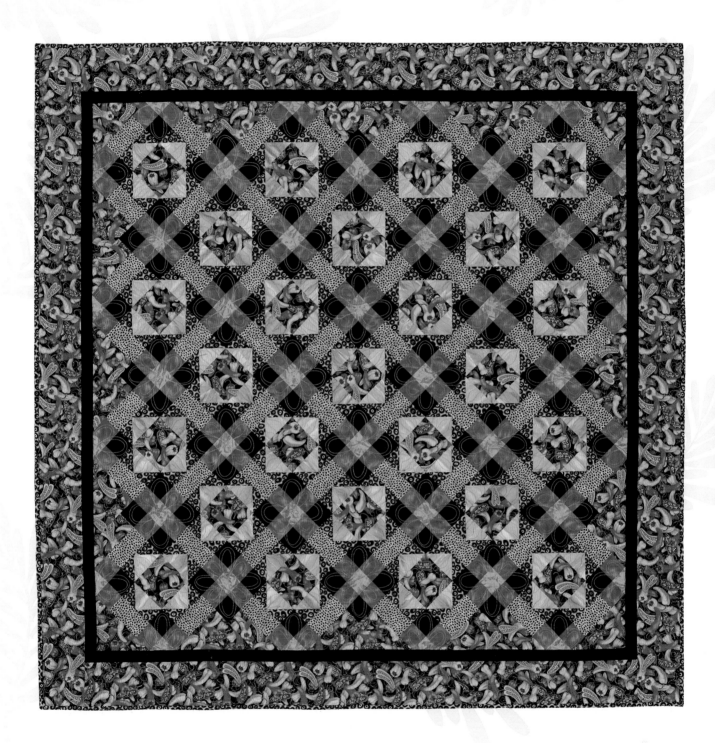

Hot Stuff

Approximate size: 68" x 68"
Made by: Nicole Chambers
Quilted by: Merline McLaughlin

When this quilt left the design wall in my studio, it was like a cloud had suddenly drifted over the room. The strong hot colors and fun personality of the hot peppers were my personal sunshine on dark and rainy winter days. It's a simple quilt to make so feel free to indulge your whimseys. Instructions on page 128.

Step-by-Step
Instructions

Shortcuts & Other Important Stuff

When you need a truckload of half square triangles ...

You can save a lot of time and effort by using the grid method to make half square triangles. This technique is both fast and reliable and makes many perfectly pieced half square triangles at one time. In my opinion, the best alternative *(as in easiest and fastest ... leaving you more time to quilt)* is to use commercially produced preprinted grids such as Triangle Paper™ or Triangles on a Roll™ rather than drawing the grid yourself.

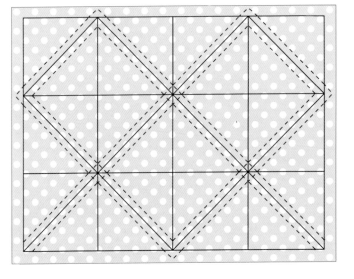

But whether you decide to draw your own grid or use one already printed for you, it's important to know that the secret to getting accurate half square triangles is to **sew accurately on the sewing lines** and **cut accurately on the cutting lines**. If you find this particularly difficult, you may want to consider making larger half square triangles than what you actually need and cutting them down to size.

But whether you are a Do-It-Yourselfer or you need a multitude of half square triangles in a size that is not commercially available, follow the simple instructions described below to draw your own grid.

Prepare your fabric by pressing the right sides of the 2 fabrics together using an iron. You may want to treat the fabrics with spray sizing to give them a little extra body and make them easier to work with. To keep things manageable, don't plan on using fabric pieces larger than 18″ x 20″ and remember to leave enough space for a margin on all the four edges.

For best results use a fine tip permanent ink marking pen and draw on the wrong side of the lighter fabric. Using the permanent ink pen and a ruler, mark a grid of squares as illustrated. The size of squares you will need to draw will be the same size that is specified in the instructions. For instance, if the instructions ask you to cut (20) $2^7/8$″ squares *(that will later become $2^1/2$″ half square triangles),* you know that you will need to draw 20 squares and that they need to be $2^7/8$″ in size *(add at least $^3/4$ to that measurement if you are making your half square triangles oversized and then trimming them down to size).*

Next, draw diagonal lines through each square on the grid. Again, refer to the illustration. With a $^1/4$ inch presser foot, sew along each side of all diagonal lines. *(Each side is sewn in one continuous seam.)*

Press stitched fabric. Using a rotary cutter and a ruler cut all squares apart. Then cut squares in half in-between the diagonal stitching lines. Gently press triangle squares open, pressing seam allowance towards the dark fabric. Trim off dog ears. Remember, accuracy in marking, sewing and cutting is crucial to making your half square triangles come out the perfect size. ■

3 Steps to Great Looking Quilts

The longer you quilt the more "tricks" you'll learn to have up your sleeve. But ultimately all of the tricks in the world won't give you the beautiful results you want if you don't follow the 3 Golden Rules of Quilting. Following these guidelines is not always glamorous, but it's this foundation that will insure your points won't get cut off; your seams will match, and your blocks will be consistently sized. In other words — you'll have quilting projects that are fun to work on and quilts you are proud to show!

1. Cut Accurately

Always take a few seconds to make sure you are measuring and cutting your fabric to the exact size specified and that your pieces are in-square. You would be amazed how many quilter think close enough is OK and then wonder why their blocks don't fit together very well and their points don't match up. How accurately you've cut your pieces is the foundation of how the entire quilt will go together. So be assured, your efforts in this area are really going to count.

Check whether the blade in your rotary cutter is still sharp before you start cutting out your quilt. It's easy to lose track of the last time the blade was replaced, and using a sharp blade will make the cutting go faster and easier as well as less tiring for your hands.

Before you start cutting strips, square up your fabric edge and then remember to resquare it after every 3 or 4 cuts *(follow this step when you are re-cutting your strips into squares and rectangles as well)*.

2. Sew Accurately

Make sure your seam allowance is consistently a scant $1/4$ inch. Double check yourself every once in a while by sewing 4 strips *(1^1/2" x 4^1/2")* together. Press seams to one side and measure. You should have a 4^1/2" x 4^1/2" square.

Thread is not the place to skimp. Use a good quality neutral colored thread and replace your sewing machine needle frequently to maintain high quality stitches.

3. Press Gently

More potentially perfect blocks get pushed and shoved out of shape at the ironing board than anywhere else. For some reason, the ironing board seems to unleash a lot of pent up emotion from even the most genteel quilters. Don't use a heavy hand or strong back and forth movements. That style of ironing will simply spell disaster for your quilt. Remind yourself to press GENTLY *(yet firmly)* with up and down movements. With a good quality iron, this technique will get the job done nicely. Take even extra care to be gentle when you are pressing pieces with raw bias edges. ■

Giving "the Pencil" the Boot!

Drawing diagonal sewing lines on fabric squares and rectangles can become tedious, not to mention boring. Do yourself a favor — run, don't walk to your favorite quilt shop and get yourself The Angler2™. For an investment of a few dollars, you will save countless hours and have the luxury of never having to draw another sewing line again *(well, almost never)*.

You can also make your own seam guide. On a piece of graph paper *(approximately 3" x 5")* mark the guide line lengthwise in the middle of the paper. Place this paper on your machine and lower the needle *(about 1" from the top end)* into the line you've drawn. Lower the presser foot. Lay a ruler *(preferably one with an ^{1}/8" grid)* against the side edge of your presser foot. Use the grid of the ruler to square up the grid of the graph paper. When you are sure your guide line is absolutely straight, secure the bottom end of your guide with tape. Cut enough off of the top end so that your feed dogs are free and the paper is not in your way.

If you don't like having a paper guide taped to your machine, you can also mark the guide by using a piece of masking tape or place the mark directly onto your machine with a permanent marker. Just be sure the guide line you are using is straight.

You can now use this guide to line up your pieces corner to corner, sewing a perfect diagonal seam without having to mark each individual piece. ■

Lynley Manor • ***A Little Romance*** *approximate size 85" x 102"*

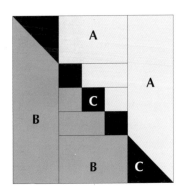

Fabric Requirements: *photos on pages 16, 32, 57, 58*

Fabric A	3¹/₂ yard
Fabric B	5²/₃*
Fabric C	2¹/₈
Fabric D	1¹/₈

*includes binding

NOTE: *These cutting instructions are based on having 40" of usable fabric width. If your fabric is even slightly wider, you may have strips left over.*

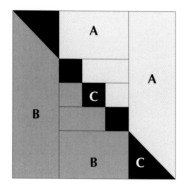

Cutting Instructions for Lynley Manor • A Little Romance

Fabric A

4 strips	1³/₄" wide	
4 strips	3" wide	Leave whole
9 strips	3" wide	Cut into (80) 3" x 4¹/₄" rectangles
20 strips	3" wide	Cut into (80) 3" x 9¹/₄" rectangles

Fabric B

4 strips	1³/₄" wide	
4 strips	3" wide	Leave whole
9 strips	3" wide	Cut into (80) 3" x 4¹/₄" rectangles
20 strips	3" wide	Cut into (80) 3" x 9¹/₄" rectangles
Outer Border		
10 strips	5¹/₂" wide	
Binding		
10 strips	2¹/₂" wide	

Fabric C

12 strips	1³/₄" wide	
14 strips	3" wide	Cut into (178) 3" squares
◣ 1 strip	3³/₈" wide	Cut into (11) 3³/₈" squares

◣ *Do NOT cut these strips if you plan on making half square triangles by drawing a grid or using products such as Triangle Paper™ or Triangles on a Roll™*

Fabric D *(Inner Border)*

◣ 1 strip	3³/₈" wide	Cut into (11) 3³/₈" squares
9 strips	3" wide	Cut into (18) 3 x 15¹/₂" rectangles

Sewing Instructions

Sew fabric A, B and C (1³/₄" and 3") strips together lengthwise as illustrated in Figure 1. Press seams as arrows indicate. Cutting across pieced strip sets, cut into 1³/₄" sections.

Figure 1

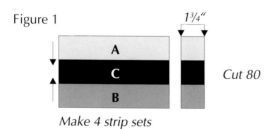

Make 4 strip sets

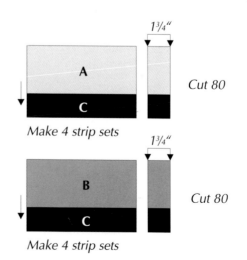

Sew sections together as illustrated in Figure 2. Press seams as arrows indicate.

IMPORTANT NOTE: *As you are working on this quilt, be sure to match the orientation of your units to those pictured in the illustrations.*

Figure 2

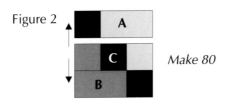

Make 80

Refer to Figure 3 and sew fabric A and B 3" x 4$\frac{1}{4}$" rectangles onto the A/B/C unit as illustrated. Press seams as arrows indicate.

Figure 3

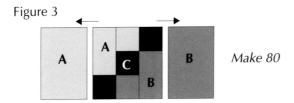

Make 80

Using a sharp pencil, draw a diagonal line on the wrong side of fabric C 3" squares *(see Shortcuts).*

Figure 4

178 fabric C 3" squares

With right sides together, position a fabric C 3" square on the corner of fabric A and B 3" x 9$\frac{1}{4}$" rectangles. Stitch on the pencil line. Press seam allowance towards outer edge and then trim to measure $\frac{1}{4}$". Refer to Figure 5.

Figure 5

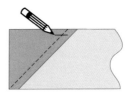

Make 80 of EACH

Sew these units onto your block as illustrated in Figure 6. Press seams as arrows indicate.

Figure 6

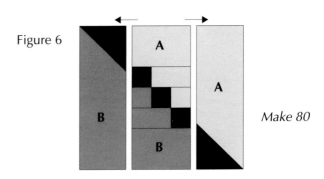

Make 80

DESIGNER TIP: *When matching diagonal seams to straight seams, mark the seam intersecting point on the diagonal seam by drawing a hatch mark $\frac{1}{4}$" from the raw edge as illustrated.*

When sewing pieces together, use this hatch mark to align intersecting seams. Place pieces right sides together and match intersecting seam points by pushing a pin straight through the intersection of the diagonal seam and hatch mark and then through the seam of the other unit. Leaving this pin straight, use other pins to secure pieces together by pinning to the right and left of the alignment pin. Remove alignment pin and sew pieces together.

Sew 4 units together as illustrated in Figure 7. Undo several stitches in the seam allowance of the pinwheel center and press seams as arrows indicate. *Do not skip this step — you'll be very glad you used this technique when you are sewing the blocks together and all of the seams butt easily.*

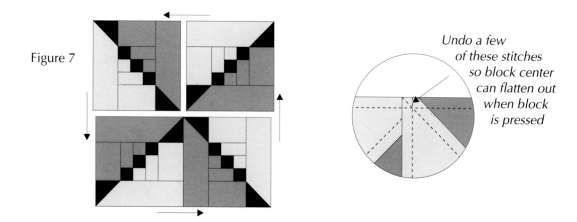

Figure 7

*Undo a few
of these stitches
so block center
can flatten out
when block
is pressed*

Inner Border

Use your favorite technique to make half square triangles or use the following method.

Place fabric C and D 3³/8" squares right sides together. Cut them in half diagonally. Sew triangles together on the wide edge. Press seam towards darker fabric and trim off dog ears. Handle bias edges carefully when you are sewing them together.

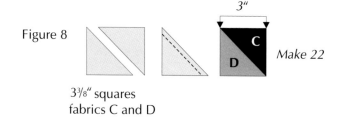

Figure 8

3"

C

D

Make 22

3³/8" squares
fabrics C and D

With right sides together, position a fabric C 3" square on the corner of a fabric D 3" x 15¹/2" rectangle. Stitch on the pencil line. Press seam allowance towards outer edge and then trim to measure ¹/4". Refer to Figure 9.

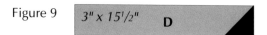

Figure 9

3" x 15¹/2"   D

Sew half square triangle and fabric C/D inner border unit together as illustrated in Figure 10. Press seam as arrow indicates.

Figure 10

Sew blocks, inner border units and the left over half square triangles to form rows as illustrated in Figure 11. Press seams in one direction, alternating that direction with every row. Sew rows together and press seams.

Figure 11

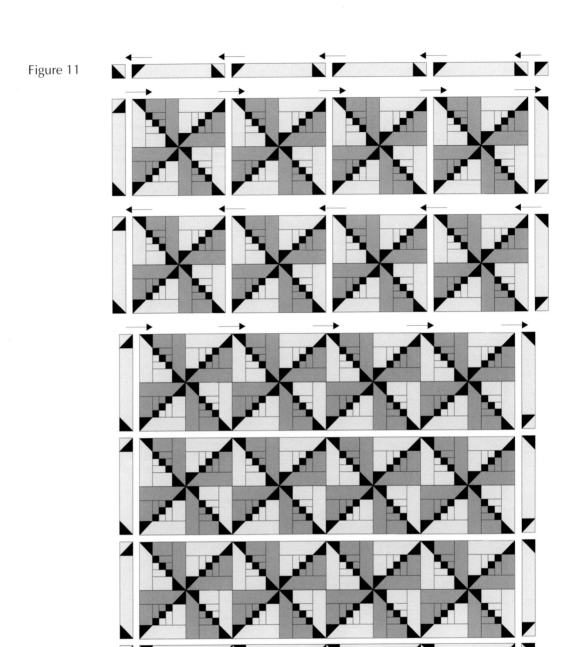

Outer Border

Measure the length of your quilt *(through the center of the quilt)* and piece 2 border strips (5$\frac{1}{2}$") to that measurement. Sew to each side of the quilt and press seams towards outer edge. Apply border to top and bottom using the same technique.

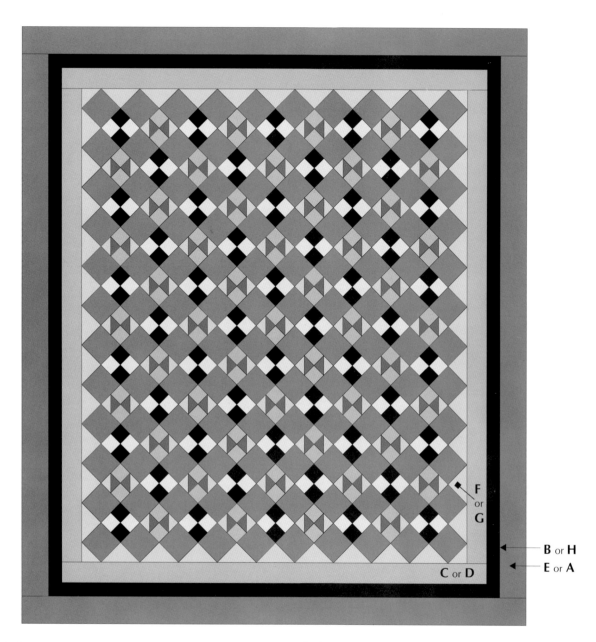

Feel the Vibe • Sassy Girl *approximate size 68" x 80"*

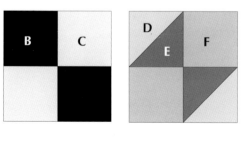

Block A   *Block B*

Fabric Requirements: *photos on pages 12, 27, 49, 50*

	Feel the Vibe	Sassy Girl
Fabric A	$2^1/8$	$2^7/8$ yards
Fabric B	$1^1/8$	$3/4$
Fabric C	$1^1/4$	$3/4$
Fabric D	$1/2$	$1^1/8$
Fabric E	$1^1/3$	$1/2$
Fabric F	$1^1/8$	$3/4$
Fabric G	—	$5/8$
Fabric H	—	$1/2$
Binding	$3/4$	$3/4$

Cutting Instructions for Feel the Vibe

NOTE: These cutting instructions are based on having 40" of usable fabric width. If your fabric is even slightly wider, you may have strips left over.

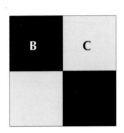

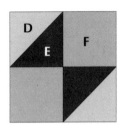

Fabric A

15 strips	$4^1/2$" wide	Cut into (120) $4^1/2$" squares

Fabric B

7 strips	$2^1/2$" wide	
8 strips	$1^1/2$" wide – *2nd border*	

Fabric C

7 strips	$2^1/2$" wide	
8 strips	$2^1/2$" wide – *1st border*	

Fabric D

◣ 4 strips	$2^7/8$" wide	Cut into (49) $2^7/8$" squares

Fabric E

◣ 4 strips	$2^7/8$" wide	Cut into (49) $2^7/8$" squares
8 strips	$3^1/4$" wide – *outer border*	

Fabric F

7 strips	$2^1/2$" wide	Cut into ((98) $2^1/2$" squares
2 strips	7" wide	Cut into (10) 7" squares cut in half diagonally twice — *setting triangles*
	scraps	(2) 4" squares cut in half diagonally once — *corner triangles*

Cutting Instructions for Sassy Girl

Fabric A

15 strips	$4^1/2$" wide	Cut into (120) $4^1/2$" squares
8 strips	$3^1/4$" wide – *outer border*	

Fabric B

7 strips	$2^1/2$" wide	

Fabric C

7 strips	$2^1/2$" wide	

◣ Do NOT cut these strips if you plan on making half square triangles by drawing a grid or using products such as Triangle Paper™ or Triangles on a Roll™

Fabric D

◣ 4 strips	$2^7/8$" wide	Cut into (49) $2^7/8$" squares
8 strips	$2^1/2$" wide – *1st border*	

Cutting Instructions
Sassy Girl

Fabric E

4 strips $2^7/8$" wide   Cut into (49) $2^7/8$" squares

Fabric F

7 strips $2^1/2$" wide   Cut into ((98) $2^1/2$" squares

Fabric G

2 strips   7" wide   Cut into (10) 7" squares cut in half
diagonally twice — *setting triangles*

scraps   (2) 4" squares cut in half diagonally
once — *corner triangles*

Fabric H

8 strips $1^1/2$" wide – *2nd border*

Binding for Feel the Vibe • Sassy Girl

8 strips $2^1/2$" wide

Sewing Instructions

Block A
Sew fabric B and C $2^1/2$" strips together lengthwise.
Press seam towards darker fabric. Cutting across
pieced strip, cut into $2^1/2$" sections.

Figure 1 $2^1/2$"

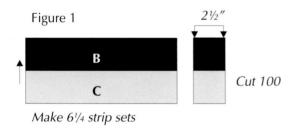

Cut 100

Make $6^1/4$ strip sets

Make a 4-patch checkerboard by sewing 2 sections
together as illustrated. Press seam as arrow indicates.

Figure 2

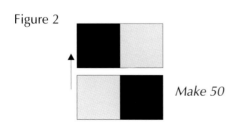

Make 50

Block B
Use your favorite technique to make half square
triangles or use the following method.

Place fabric D and E $2^7/8$" squares right sides together.
Cut them in half diagonally. Sew triangles together on
the wide edge. Press seam towards darker fabric and
trim off dog ears.

Figure 3 $2^1/2$"

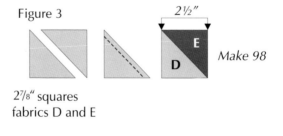

Make 98

$2^7/8$" squares
fabrics D and E

HINT: *When making a large number of half square
triangles, the grid method (see Shortcuts) makes this
job fast, easy and accurate.*

Sew half square triangles and fabric F 2¹/₂" squares together as illustrated in Figure 4. Press seam as arrow indicates.

Figure 4

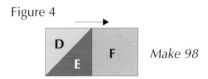

Make 98

Sew units together as illustrated in Figure 5. Press seam as arrow indicates.

Figure 5

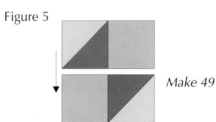

Make 49

Arrange blocks A, B, fabric A 4¹/₂" squares, setting triangles and corner triangles *(fabric F or G)* as illustrated in Figure 6. Sew pieces together to form diagonal rows. Press seams as arrows indicate. Sew rows together and press.

Border

Measure the length of your quilt *(through the center of your quilt)* and piece 2 fabric A or E *(1st border)* strips to that measurement. Sew to each side of the quilt and press towards outer edge.

Apply border to top and bottom of the quilt using the same technique.

Repeat these steps for 2nd border *(fabric B or H)* and then again for the outer border *(fabric E or A)*.

IMPORTANT NOTE: *If you are using a striped or directional fabric for the fabric A 4¹/₂" squares, use the white arrows in Figure 6 to guide you in which direction the stripes should run.*

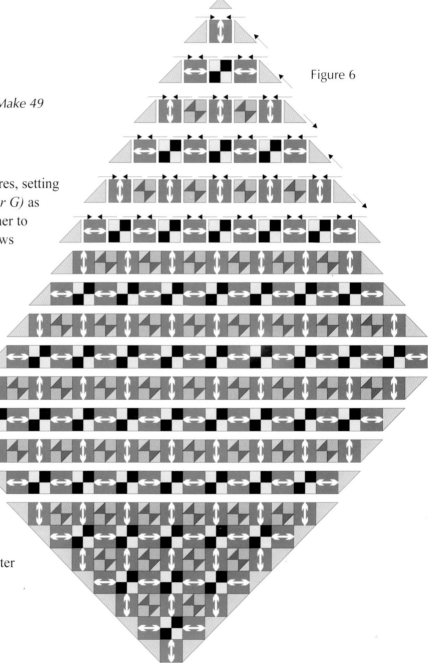

Figure 6

Samurai Garden *approximate size 64" x 72"*

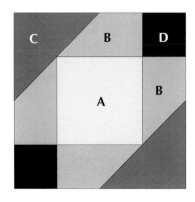

Fabric Requirements: *photos on pages 22, 46*

Fabric A	$2^{1}/_{2}$* yards
Fabric B	$2^{5}/_{8}$
Fabric C	2
Fabric D	$^{3}/_{4}$

Includes binding

NOTE: These cutting instructions are based on having 40" of usable fabric width. If your fabric is even slightly wider, you may have strips left over.

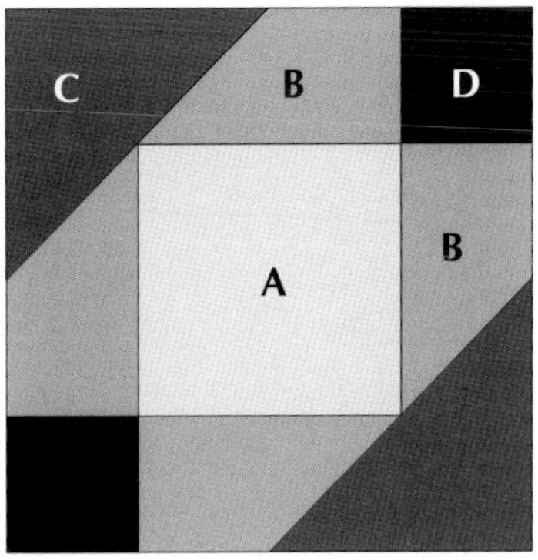
C
B
D
B
A

Cutting Instructions for Samurai Garden

Fabric A

7 strips	4½" wide	
Border		
7 strips	4½" wide	
Binding		
7 strips	2½" wide	

Fabric B

14 strips	2½" wide	
7 strips	6½" wide	
1 strip	4⅞" wide	Cut into (1) 4⅞" square *and* (2) 2½" x 4½" rectangles

Fabric C

13 strips	4½" wide	Cut into (110) 4½" squares
1 strip	4⅞" wide	(1) 4⅞" square — *after cutting this square trim remaining strip to 4½" and cut into 4½" squares*

Fabric D

7 strips	2½" wide	

Sewing Instructions

With right sides together, sew fabric B 2½" strips and fabric A 4½" strip together lengthwise as illustrated in Figure 1A. Press seams as arrows indicate. Cutting across pieced strip sets, cut into 4½" and 2½" sections.

Figure 1A

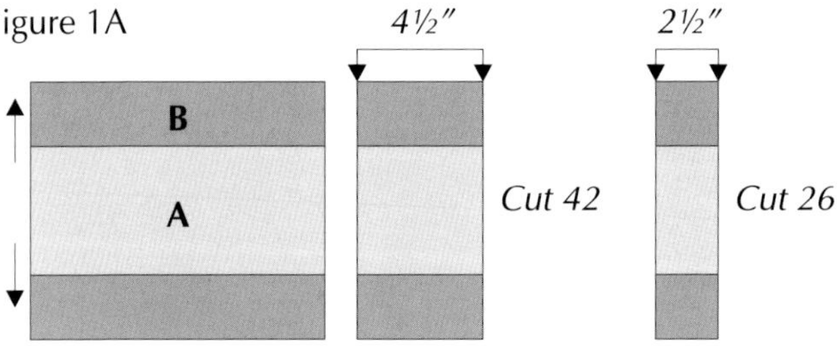
4½"
2½"
B
A
Cut 42
Cut 26

Make 7 strip sets

With right sides together, sew fabric D 2½" strip and fabric B 6½" strip together lengthwise and cut into 2½" sections. Refer to Figure 1B.

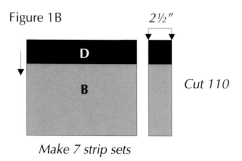

Figure 1B

2½"

D

B

Cut 110

Make 7 strip sets

Sew fabric B/D units onto fabric A/B units as illustrated in Figure 2. Press seams as arrows indicate.

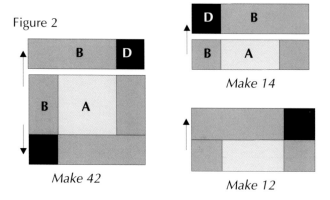

Figure 2

B D

B A

Make 42

D B

B A

Make 14

Make 12

Place fabric B and C 4⅞" squares right sides together. Cut them in half diagonally. Sew triangles together on the wide edge. Press seams towards darker fabric and trim off dog ears. Handle bias edges carefully when you are sewing them together.

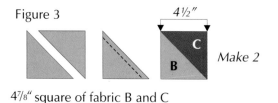

Figure 3

4½"

C

B

Make 2

4⅞" square of fabric B and C

Take remaining 2 fabric B/D units and trim fabric B end so it measures 2¼" from seam. Refer to Figure 4.

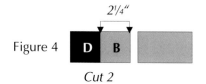

2¼"

Figure 4

D B

Cut 2

Sew a fabric B 2½" x 4½" rectangle onto side of trimmed B/D unit as illustrated in Figure 5. Press seam as arrow indicates.

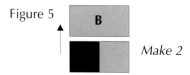

Figure 5

B

Make 2

With WRONG sides together, press fabric C 4½" squares in half diagonally *(you will use this fold as a sewing guide so be sure it is folded accurately)*. Place the folded triangle on the block making sure triangle is not cutting off corners on the center fabric A square. Coax it into place if necessary. Open square and pin to secure. Sew on the fold line. Press seam allowance towards outer edge and then trim to measure ¼". Repeat these steps for the other corner. Refer to Figure 6.

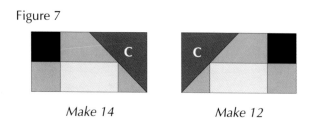

Figure 6

Make 42

C

Repeating these steps, add fabric C triangle to the units illustrated in Figure 7.

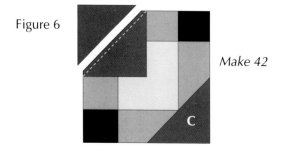

Figure 7

C

Make 14

C

Make 12

Mark seam intersections on the wrong side of blocks by drawing hatch marks ¼" from the edge as illustrated in Figure 8.

HINT: When sewing blocks together, use these hatch marks to align intersecting seams. Place blocks right sides together and match intersecting seam points by pushing a pin straight through the intersection of diagonal seam and hatch mark of both blocks. Leaving this pin straight, use other pins to secure pieces together by pinning to the right and left of the alignment pin. Remove alignment pin and sew blocks together.

Figure 8

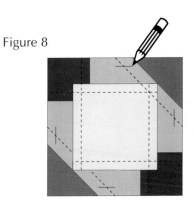

Mark ¼" seam intersections

Sew blocks together to make rows as illustrated in Figure 9. Press seams in the direction arrows indicate. Use the hatch marks as seam match points and pin intersecting seams before sewing.

Sew rows together, alternating rows A and B so seams butt together. Press quilt.

Figure 9

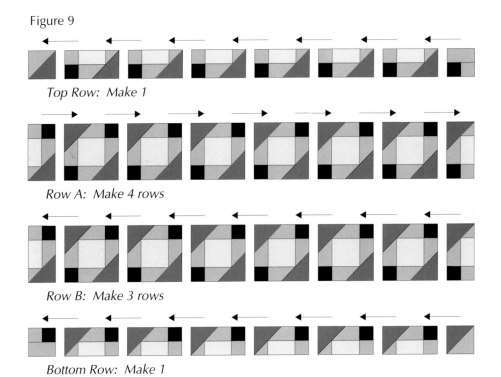

Top Row: Make 1

Row A: Make 4 rows

Row B: Make 3 rows

Bottom Row: Make 1

Border
Measure the length of your quilt *(through the center of your quilt)* and piece 2 fabric A (4½") border strips to that measurement. Sew to each side of the quilt and press towards outer edge.

Apply border to top and bottom of the quilt using the same technique.

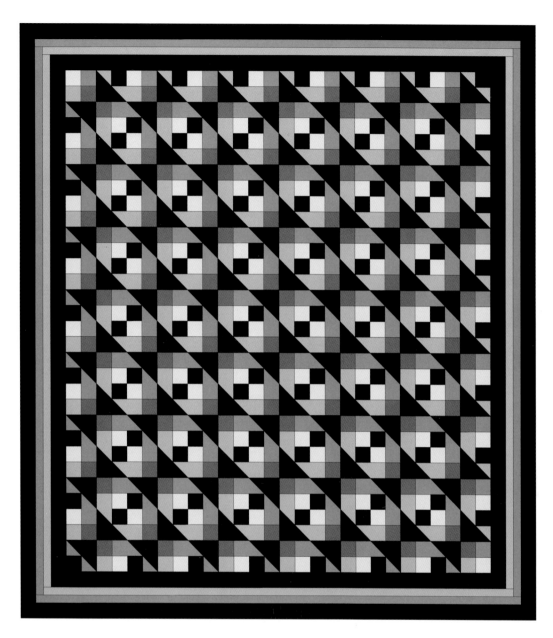

Alternating Currents *approximate size 68" x 76"*

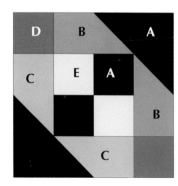

Fabric Requirements: *photos on pages 11, 45*

Fabric A	$4^3/8$ yards*
Fabric B	$1^3/4$
Fabric C	$1^3/4$
Fabric D	$5/8$
Fabric E	$5/8$

Includes border and binding

Cutting Instructions for Alternating Currents

NOTE: *These cutting instructions are based on having 40" of usable fabric width. If your fabric is even slightly wider, you may have strips left over.*

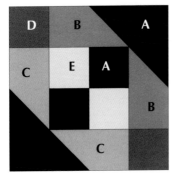

Fabric A

14 strips	4^1/$_2$" wide	Cut into (112) 4^1/$_2$" squares
7 strips	2^1/$_2$" wide	
	scraps	(2) 2^1/$_2$" squares
Border		
7 strips	2^1/$_2$" wide *(inner border)*	
8 strips	3^1/$_2$" wide *(outer border)*	
Binding		
8 strips	2^1/$_2$" wide	

Fabric B

4 strips	6^1/$_2$" wide	
3 strips	4^1/$_2$" wide	Cut into (43) 4^1/$_2$" x 2^1/$_2$" rectangles
2 strips	2^1/$_2$" wide	Cut into (29) 2^1/$_2$" squares
Border		
7 strips	1^1/$_2$" wide	

Fabric C

4 strips	6^1/$_2$" wide	
3 strips	4^1/$_2$" wide	Cut into (43) 4^1/$_2$" x 2^1/$_2$" rectangles
2 strips	2^1/$_2$" wide	Cut into (29) 2^1/$_2$" squares
Border		
7 strips	1^1/$_2$" wide	

Fabric D

7 strips	2^1/$_2$" wide	
	scraps	(2) 2^1/$_2$" squares

Fabric E

7 strips	2^1/$_2$" wide	
	scraps	(2) 2^1/$_2$" squares

Sewing Instructions

With right sides together, sew fabric A and E 2^1/$_2$" strips together lengthwise as illustrated in Figure 1. Press seam as arrow indicates. Cutting across pieced strip set, cut into 2^1/$_2$" sections.

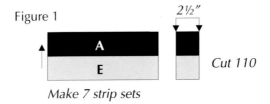

Figure 1

2½"

Cut 110

Make 7 strip sets

Make a 4-patch checkerboard by sewing 2 sections together as illustrated in Figure 2.

Figure 2

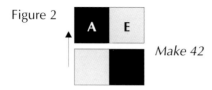

Make 42

Add fabric B and C 2$\frac{1}{2}$" x 4$\frac{1}{2}$" rectangles to sides of the 4-patch as illustrated in Figure 3. Press as arrows indicate.

NOTE: *Be sure to match the fabric orientation of your pieces to the illustrations.*

Figure 3

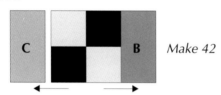

Make 42

With right sides together, sew fabric D 2$\frac{1}{2}$" strips onto fabric B and C 6$\frac{1}{2}$" strips as illustrated in Figure 4. Press seams as arrows indicate. Cutting across pieced strip sets, cut into 2$\frac{1}{2}$" sections.

Figure 4

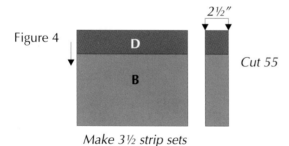

2$\frac{1}{2}$"

Cut 55

Make 3½ strip sets

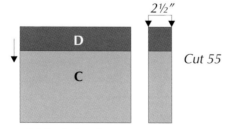

2$\frac{1}{2}$"

Cut 55

Make 3½ strip sets

Refer to Figure 5 and sew sections onto top and bottom of the block as illustrated. Press seams as arrows indicate.

Figure 5

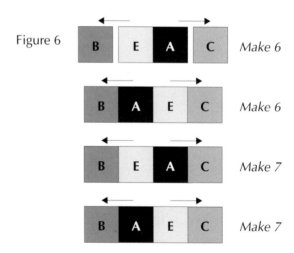

Make 42

Refer to Figure 6 and add fabric B and C 2$\frac{1}{2}$" squares to fabric A/E units as illustrated. Press seams as arrows indicate.

Figure 6

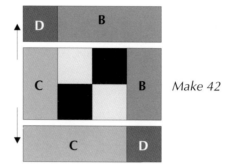

Make 6

Make 6

Make 7

Make 7

Refer to Figure 7 and sew fabric B/D and C/D sections onto these units as illustrated.

Figure 7

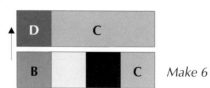

Make 6

Figure 7 *continued*

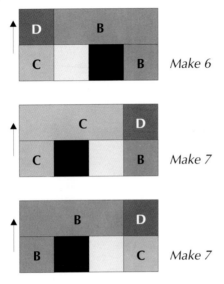

Make 6

Make 7

Make 7

To make corner units, sew pieces together as illustrated in Figure 8. Press seams as arrows indicate.

Figure 8

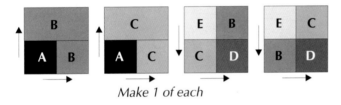

Make 1 of each

With WRONG sides together, press fabric A 4½" squares in half diagonally *(you will use the fold as a sewing guide so be sure it is folded accurately)*. Place the folded triangle on the block making sure triangle is not cutting off corners on the 4-patch. Coax it into place if necessary. Open square and pin to secure. Sew on the fold line. Press seam allowance towards outer edge and then trim to measure ¼". Repeat these steps for the other corner. Refer to Figure 9.

Figure 9

Make 42

Repeating these steps, add fabric A triangle to the units illustrated in Figure 10.

Figure 10

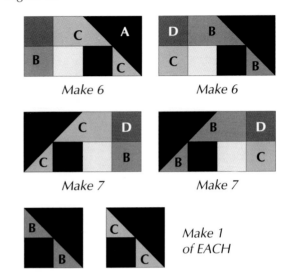

Make 6   *Make 6*

Make 7   *Make 7*

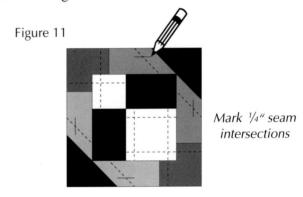

Make 1 of EACH

Mark seam intersections on the wrong side of blocks by drawing hatch marks ¼" from the edge as illustrated in Figure 11.

Figure 11

Mark ¼" seam intersections

HINT: *When sewing blocks together, use these hatch marks to align intersecting seams. Place blocks right sides together and match intersecting seam points by pushing a pin straight through the intersection of diagonal seam and hatch mark of both blocks. Leaving this pin straight, use other pins to secure pieces together by pinning to the right and left of the alignment pin. Remove alignment pin and sew blocks together.*

Sew blocks together to make rows as illustrated in Figure 12. Press seams in the direction arrows indicate. Use the hatch marks as seam match points and pin intersecting seams before sewing.

Sew rows together, alternating rows A and B so seams butt together. Press quilt.

Figure 12

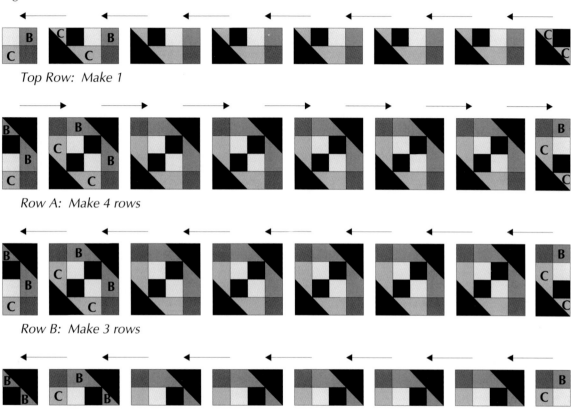

Top Row: Make 1

Row A: Make 4 rows

Row B: Make 3 rows

Bottom Row: Make 1

Borders
Measure the length of your quilt *(through the center of your quilt)* and piece 2 fabric A (2¹/2") border strips to that measurement. Sew to each side of the quilt and press towards outer edge.

Apply border to top and bottom of the quilt using the same technique.

Repeat these steps for fabric C 1¹/2" border strips and then again for fabric B 1¹/2" border strips.

Repeat again for fabric A 3¹/2" outer border.

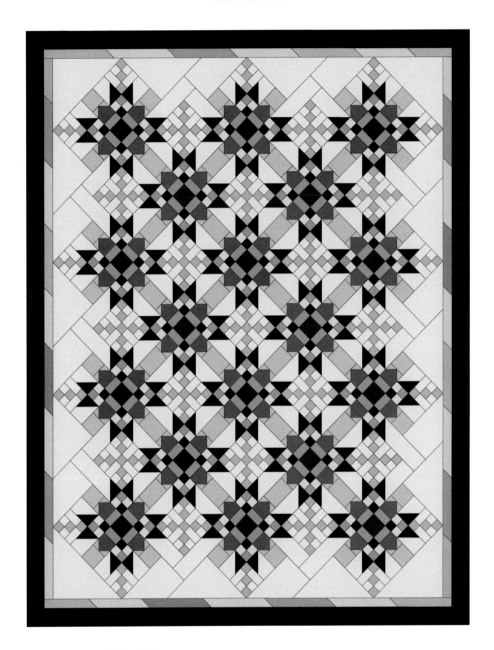

Morning Star *approximate size 85" x 108"*

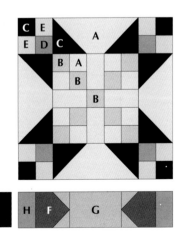

Fabric Requirements: *photos on pages 20, 43*

Fabric A	5 yards
Fabric B	1
Fabric C	3³/₄*
Fabric D	⁵/₈
Fabric E	⁵/₈
Fabric F	1¹/₈
Fabric G	1¹/₄
Fabric H	⁷/₈
Fabric I	⁵/₈

Includes outer border and binding

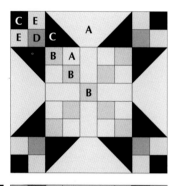

NOTE: *These cutting instructions are based on having 40" of usable fabric width. If your fabric is even slightly wider, you may have strips left over.*

Cutting Instructions for Morning Star

Fabric A

9 strips	2" wide	
24 strips	$3^{1}/2$" wide	Leave 2 strips whole
		Cut remaining strips into:

                (10) 11" x $3^{1}/2$" rectangles
                (58) 8" x $3^{1}/2$" rectangles
                (28) 5" x $3^{1}/2$" rectangles
                (65) 2" x $3^{1}/2$" rectangles

Setting & corner triangles

3 strips	$16^{1}/4$" wide	Cut into (5) $16^{1}/4$" squares cut in half diagonally twice — *setting triangles*
1 strip	$13^{3}/4$" wide	Cut into (2) $13^{3}/4$" squares cut in half diagonally once — *corner triangles*

Fabric B

11 strips	2" wide	

Pieced border

2 strips	$2^{1}/2$" wide	Cut into (8) $2^{1}/2$" x 10" rectangles

---

Fabric C

14 strips	$3^{1}/2$" wide	Cut into (144) $3^{1}/2$" squares
4 strips	2" wide	

Outer border

10 strips	$4^{1}/2$" wide	

Binding

10 strips	$2^{1}/2$" wide	

Fabric D

4 strips	2" wide	

Pieced border

2 strips	$2^{1}/2$" wide	Cut into (8) $2^{1}/2$" x 10" rectangles

---

Fabric E

8 strips	2" wide	

Fabric F

7 strips	$3^{1}/2$" wide	

Pieced border

2 strips	$2^{1}/2$" wide	Cut into (8) $2^{1}/2$" x 10" rectangles

---

Cutting Instructions

Morning Star

Fabric G

8 strips	2" wide	Cut into (144) 2" squares
6 strips	3¹/2" wide	Cut into (24) 5" x 3¹/2" rectangles *and* (24) 3¹/2" squares

Fabric H

7 strips	2" wide	
Pieced border		
3 strips	2¹/2" wide	Cut into (12) 2¹/2" x 10" rectangles

Fabric I

2 strips	3¹/2" wide	Cut into (18) 3¹/2" squares
Pieced border		
3 strips	2¹/2" wide	Cut into (12) 2¹/2" x 10" rectangles

Freezer paper	(10) 2" x 7" rectangles

Sewing Instructions

With right sides together, sew fabric A and B 2" strips together lengthwise. Press seam as arrow indicates. Cutting across the pieced strip, cut into 2" sections.

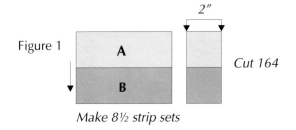

Figure 1 — *Make 8½ strip sets* — Cut 164

Make a 4-patch checkerboard by sewing 2 sections together as illustrated in Figure 2. Press seam as arrow indicates.

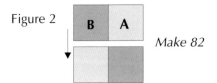

Figure 2 — *Make 82*

HINT: *To achieve a nicely joined seam intersection, nestle intersecting seams together before sewing. Do NOT place a pin at the intersecting point.*

With right sides together, sew fabric A 3¹/₂" strip and fabric B 2" strip together lengthwise. Press seam as arrow indicates. Cutting across the pieced strip, cut into 2" sections.

Figure 3

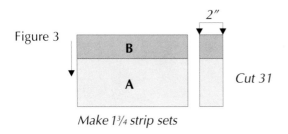

Cut 31

Make 1³/₄ strip sets

Sew pieced units and fabric A 2" x 3¹/₂" rectangles together as illustrated in Figure 4. Press seams as arrows indicate.

Figure 4

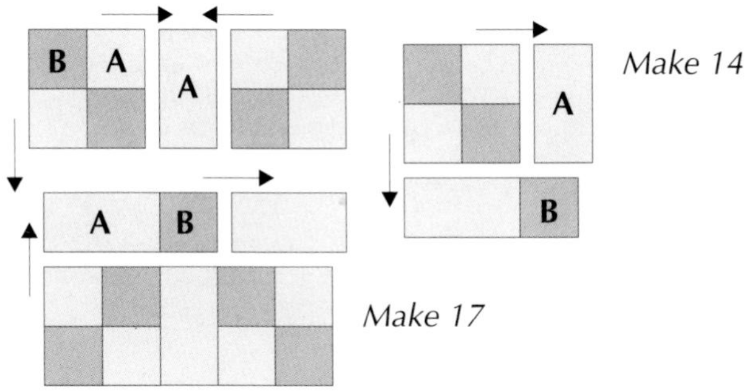

Make 14

Make 17

Draw a diagonal line on the wrong side of fabric C 3¹/₂" squares *(see Shortcuts).*

Figure 5

144 fabric C 3½" squares

With right sides together, position a fabric C 3¹/₂" square on the corner of fabric A rectangles (8" x 3¹/₂", 11" x 3¹/₂" and 5" x 3¹/₂") as illustrated in Figure 6. Stitch on the pencil line. Press seam allowance towards outer edge and then trim to measure ¹/₄".

Figure 6

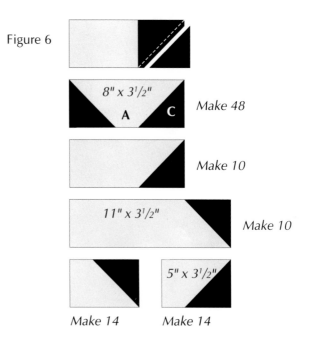

8" x 3¹/₂"

A   C   *Make 48*

Make 10

11" x 3¹/₂"   *Make 10*

5" x 3¹/₂"

Make 14   *Make 14*

Sew Fabric C, D and E 2" strips together lengthwise as illustrated in Figure 7. Press seams as arrows indicate. Cutting across the pieced strips, cut into 2" sections.

Figure 7

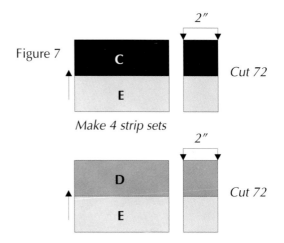

C   *Cut 72*

E

Make 4 strip sets

D   *Cut 72*

E

Make a 4-patch checkerboard by sewing sections together as illustrated in Figure 8. Press seam as arrow indicates.

Figure 8

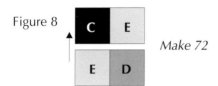

Make 72

Sew 4-patch units and fabric A/C units together as illustrated in Figure 9. Press seams as arrows indicate.

Figure 9

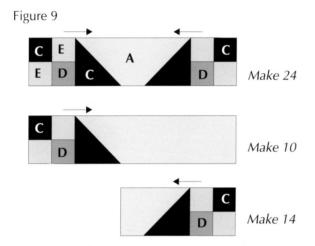

Make 24

Make 10

Make 14

Refer to Figure 10 and sew units together as illustrated. Press seams as arrows indicate.

Figure 10

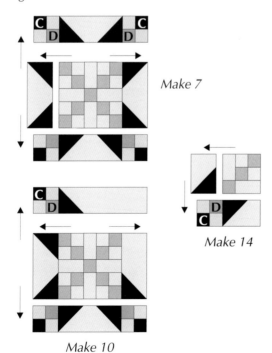

Make 7

Make 14

Make 10

DESIGNER TIP: *When matching diagonal seams to straight seams, mark the seam intersecting point on the diagonal seam by drawing a hatch mark $^1/4"$ from the raw edge as illustrated.*

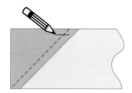

When sewing pieces together, use this hatch mark to align intersecting seams. Place pieces right sides together and match intersecting seam points by pushing a pin straight through the intersection of the diagonal seam and hatch mark and then through the seam of the other unit. Leaving this pin straight, use other pins to secure pieces together by pinning to the right and left of the alignment pin. Remove alignment pin and sew pieces together.

With right sides together, sew fabric F $3^1/2"$ strip and Fabric H 2" strip together lengthwise. Press seam as arrow indicates. Cutting across the pieced strip, cut into $3^1/2"$ sections.

Figure 11

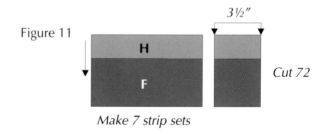

$3^1/2"$

Cut 72

Make 7 strip sets

Draw a diagonal line on the wrong side of all fabric G 2" squares *(see Shortcuts)*.

Figure 12

144 fabric G 2" squares

With right sides together, position a fabric G 2" square on the corner of a fabric F/H unit. Stitch on the pencil line. Press seam allowance towards the outer edge and cut seam to measure ¼". Repeat these steps for the other corner. Refer to Figure 13.

Figure 13

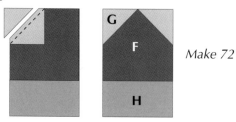

Make 72

Sew fabric F/G/H units, fabric G rectangles and squares together as illustrated in Figure 14. Press seams as arrows indicate.

Figure 14

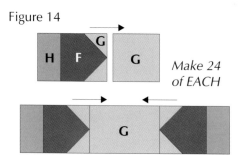

Make 24 of EACH

Trim 10 setting triangles as illustrated in Figure 15. Using a DRY iron, press shiny side of freezer paper onto WRONG side of trimmed triangle. This will stabilize bias edge. Freezer paper will be removed when rows are being pinned together.

_____

IMPORTANT NOTE: *If you want to trim several triangles at the same time be sure to stack them RIGHT side up before cutting them.*

_____

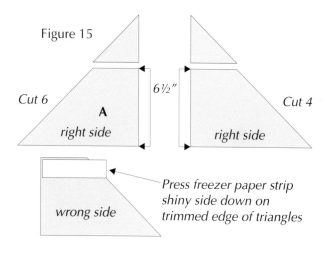

Figure 15

Cut 6   6½"   Cut 4

A right side   right side

Press freezer paper strip shiny side down on trimmed edge of triangles

wrong side

Refer to Figure 16 and sew pieces together as illustrated. Press seams as arrows indicate.

Figure 16

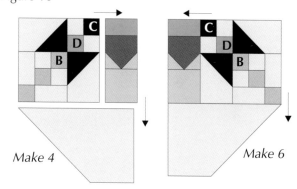

Make 4   Make 6

Refer to Figure 17 and begin by sewing sashing units in-between blocks. Next sew sashing units and fabric I (3½") squares together. Press seams as arrows indicate.

Sew block row and sashing row together to form unit as illustrated. Press seam towards sashing as arrow indicates.

Refer to Figure 18 and add setting triangles as indicated. Press seams towards setting triangles.

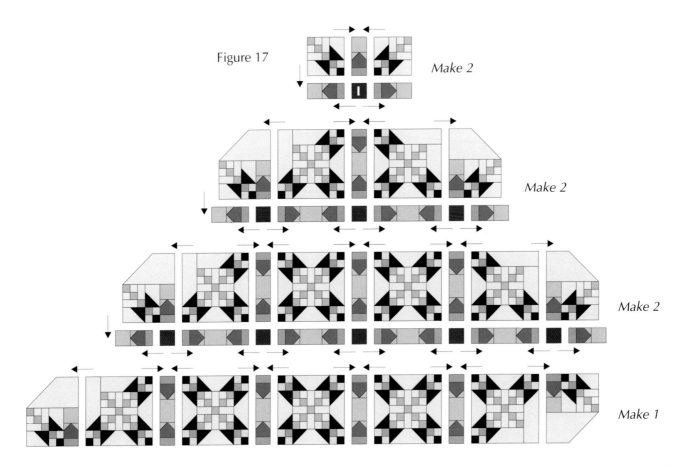

Figure 17

Make 2

Make 2

Make 2

Make 1

Arrange rows as illustrated in Figure 18. Handling quilt carefully, sew rows together. Freezer paper can be removed while pinning rows together or after they've been sewn together. Add corner triangles and press.

Pieced Border

On the wrong side of 2½" x 10" border strips, draw a hatch mark 2½" from one end. Simply place 2 rectangles at right angles to each other matching the top edge and mark as illustrated in Figure 19.

Figure 19

46 assorted
2½" x 10" rectangles

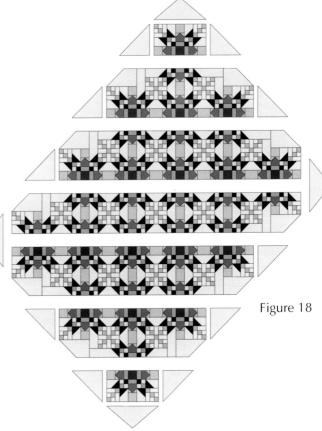

Figure 18

Draw a diagonal line from the outer corner to this mark as illustrated in Figure 20 *(see Shortcuts)*.

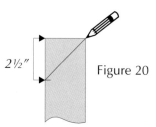

2½"   Figure 20

To make diagonal seams, layer rectangles right sides together as illustrated in Figure 21. Sew on the pencil line. Sew rectangles together in this manner varying fabric colors. Press seam allowance in one direction and then trim to measure ¼".

For pieced border sides, sew 13 rectangles together and for the top and bottom, sew 10 rectangles together. Keep your diagonal seams slanting in the same direction.

Figure 21

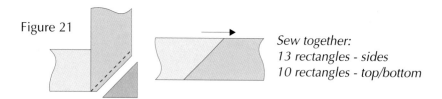

Sew together:
13 rectangles - sides
10 rectangles - top/bottom

Measure the length of your quilt (*through the center of the quilt*) and trim pieced side borders to that measurement. Sew to each side of the quilt and press seam towards outer edge. Apply pieced borders to top and bottom using the same technique. ***Pay particular attention to the direction of the diagonal seams when you are sewing the border strips onto the quilt.***

HINT: *To trim pieced borders so they are even on both ends, fold border units in half, wrong sides together. Starting at the fold, measure HALF of the quilt length (or width) measurement and trim off excess fabric.*

Add fabric C outer border strips (4½") by first applying them to quilt sides and then to quilt top and bottom.

K   H   G   H   K   H

Mysteries of the Night *approximate size 81" x 81"*

Fabric Requirements: *photos on pages 6, 44*

Fabric A	4 yards
Fabric B	$^2/_3$
Fabric C	$1^1/_4$
Fabric D	$^1/_2$
Fabric E	$^1/_4$
Fabric F	$^1/_4$
Fabric G	1
Fabric H	$1^7/_8$
Fabric I	$^1/_2$
Fabric J	$^3/_8$
Fabric K	$1^5/_8$ *(border and binding)*

NOTE: *These cutting instructions are based on having 40" of usable fabric width. If your fabric is even slightly wider, you may have strips left over.*

Cutting Instructions for Mysteries of the Night

Fabric A

6 strips	2" wide	
18 strips	$3^1/2$" wide	Leave $1^1/2$ strips whole

Cut remaining strips into:

(8) 11" x $3^1/2$" rectangles
(40) 8" x $3^1/2$" rectangles
(24) 5" x $3^1/2$" rectangles
(48) 2" x $3^1/2$" rectangles

Setting & corner triangles

2 strips	$16^1/4$" wide	Cut into (4) $16^1/4$" squares cut in half diagonally twice — *setting triangles*
1 strip	$13^3/4$" wide	Cut into (2) $13^3/4$" squares cut in half diagonally once — *corner triangles*

Fabric B

8 strips	2" wide

Fabric C

10 strips	$3^1/2$" wide	Cut into (104) $3^1/2$" squares

Fabric D

6 strips	2" wide

Fabric E

3 strips	2" wide

Fabric F

3 strips	2" wide

Fabric G

5 strips	$3^1/2$" wide

Pieced border

2 strips	$4^1/2$" wide	Cut into (8) 9" x $4^1/2$" rectangles

Fabric H

6 strips	2" wide	Cut into (104) 2" squares
4 strips	$3^1/2$" wide	Cut into (16) 5 x $3^1/2$" rectangles *and* (20) $3^1/2$" squares

Cutting Instructions

Mysteries of the Night

Fabric H *continued*
Pieced border

7 strips	4¹/₂" wide	Cut into (8) 13" x 4¹/₂" rectangles *and* (16) 9" x 4¹/₂" rectangles

Fabric I

5 strips	2" wide

Fabric J

2 strips	3¹/₂" wide	Cut into (13) 3¹/₂" squares

Fabric K

6 strips	4¹/₂" wide	Cut into (4) 19" x 4¹/₂" rectangles *and* (8) 15¹/₂" x 4¹/₂" rectangles — *border*

Binding

9 strips	2¹/₂" wide

Freezer paper   (8) 2" x 7" rectangles

Sewing Instructions

With right sides together, sew fabric A and B 2" strips together lengthwise. Press seam as arrow indicates. Cutting across the pieced strip, cut into 2" sections.

Figure 1

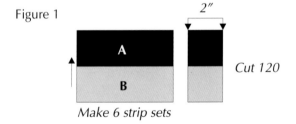

Cut 120

Make 6 strip sets

Make a 4-patch checkerboard by sewing 2 sections together as illustrated in Figure 2. Press seam as arrow indicates.

Figure 2

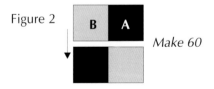

Make 60

HINT: *To achieve a nicely joined seam intersection, nestle intersecting seams together before sewing. Do NOT place a pin at the intersecting point.*

With right sides together, sew fabric A 3¹/₂" strip and fabric B 2" strip together lengthwise. Press seam as arrow indicates. Cutting across the pieced strip, cut into 2" sections.

Figure 3

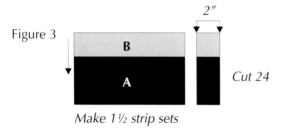

Cut 24

Make 1 ½ strip sets

Sew pieced units and fabric A 2" x 3¹/₂" rectangles together as illustrated in Figure 4. Press seams as arrows indicate.

Figure 4

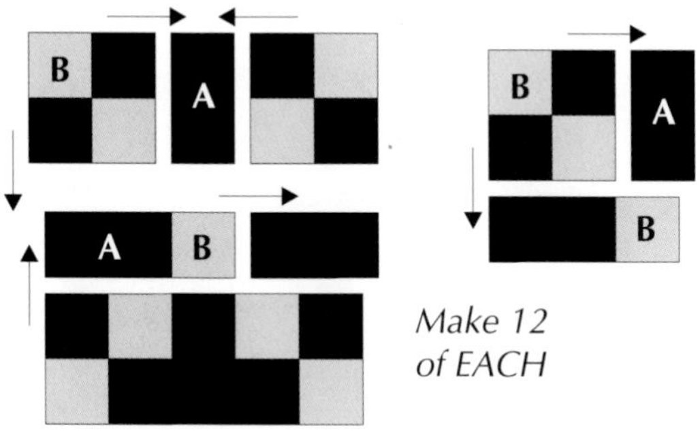

Make 12 of EACH

Draw a diagonal line on the wrong side of fabric C 3¹/₂" squares *(see Shortcuts)*.

Figure 5

104 fabric C 3½" squares

With right sides together, position a fabric C 3¹/₂" square on the corner of fabric A rectangles (8" x 3¹/₂", 11" x 3¹/₂" and 5" x 3¹/₂") as illustrated in Figure 6. Stitch on the pencil line. Press seam allowance towards outer edge and then trim to measure ¹/₄".

Figure 6

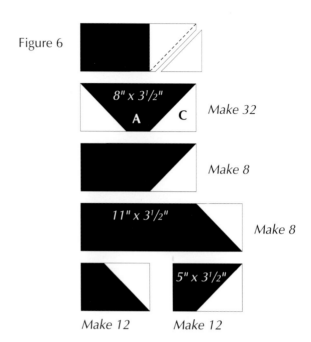

8" x 3¹/₂"

A   C   *Make 32*

Make 8

11" x 3¹/₂"   *Make 8*

5" x 3¹/₂"

Make 12   *Make 12*

Sew fabric D, E and F 2" strips together lengthwise as illustrated in Figure 7. Press seams as arrows indicate. Cutting across the pieced strips, cut into 2" sections.

Figure 7

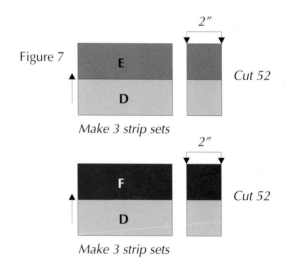

E

D

Cut 52

Make 3 strip sets

F

D

Cut 52

Make 3 strip sets

Make a 4-patch checkerboard by sewing sections together as illustrated in Figure 8. Press seam as arrow indicates.

Figure 8

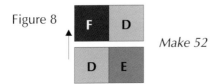

Make 52

Sew fabric D/E/F 4-patch and fabric A/C units together as illustrated in Figure 9. Press seams as arrows indicate.

Figure 9

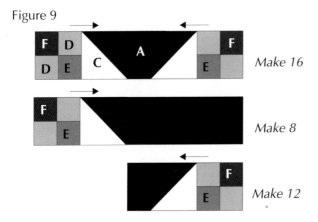

Make 16

Make 8

Make 12

Refer to Figure 10 and sew units together as illustrated. Press seams as arrows indicate.

Figure 10

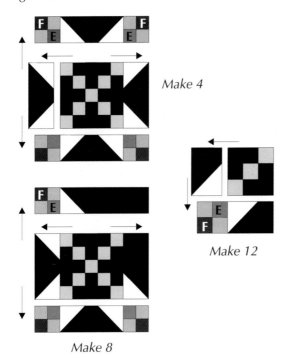

Make 4

Make 12

Make 8

DESIGNER TIP: *When matching diagonal seams to straight seams, mark the seam intersecting point on the diagonal seam by drawing a hatch mark $^1/_4$" from the raw edge as illustrated.*

When sewing pieces together, use this hatch mark to align intersecting seams. Place pieces right sides together and match intersecting seam points by pushing a pin straight through the intersection of the diagonal seam and hatch mark and then through the seam of the other unit. Leaving this pin straight, use other pins to secure pieces together by pinning to the right and left of the alignment pin. Remove alignment pin and sew pieces together.

With right sides together, sew fabric G (3$^1/_2$") strip and fabric I (2") strip together lengthwise. Press seam as arrow indicates. Cutting across the pieced strip, cut into 3$^1/_2$" sections.

Figure 11

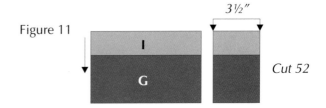

3½"

Cut 52

Draw a diagonal line on the wrong side of all fabric H 2" squares *(see Shortcuts)*.

Figure 12

104 fabric H 2" squares

With right sides together, position a fabric H 2" square on the corner of fabric G/I unit. Stitch on the pencil line. Press seam allowance towards the outer edge and cut seam to measure ¼". Repeat these steps for the other corner. Refer to Figure 13.

Figure 13

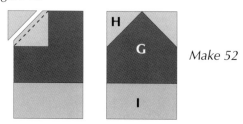

Make 52

Sew fabric G/H/I units, fabric H rectangles and squares together as illustrated in Figure 14. Press seams as arrows indicate.

Figure 14

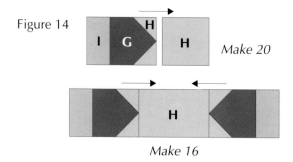

Make 20

Make 16

Trim 8 setting triangles as illustrated in Figure 15. Using a DRY iron, press shiny side of freezer paper onto WRONG side of trimmed triangle. This will stabilize bias edge. Freezer paper will be removed when rows are being pinned together.

IMPORTANT NOTE: *If you want to trim several triangles at the same time, be sure to stack them RIGHT side up before cutting them.*

Figure 15

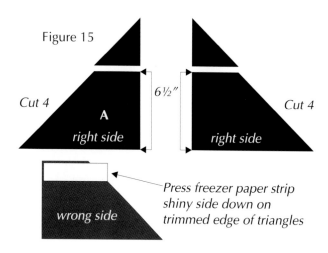

Cut 4   Cut 4

6½"

A right side   right side

Press freezer paper strip shiny side down on trimmed edge of triangles

wrong side

Refer to Figure 16 and sew pieces together as illustrated. Press seams as arrows indicate.

Figure 16

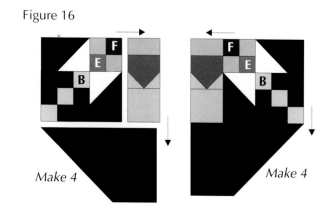

Make 4   *Make 4*

Refer to Figure 17 and begin by sewing sashing units in-between blocks. Next sew sashing units and fabric J 3½" squares together. Press seams as arrows indicate.

Sew block row and sashing row together to form unit as illustrated. Press seam towards sashing as arrow indicates.

Refer to Figure 18 and add setting triangles as indicated. Press seams towards setting triangles.

Figure 17

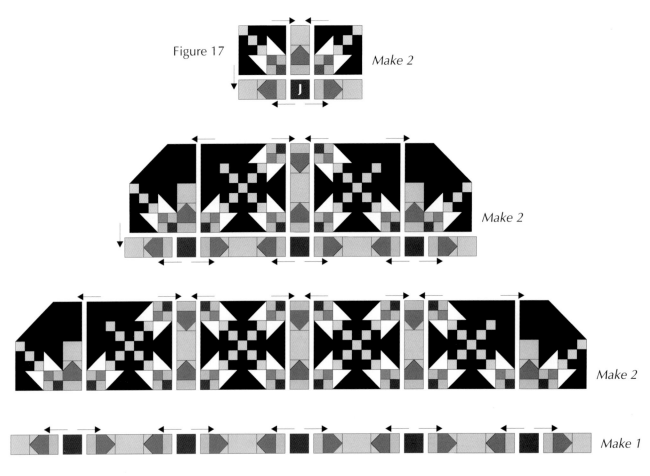

Make 2

Make 2

Make 2

Make 1

Arrange rows as illustrated in Figure 18. Handling quilt carefully, sew rows together. Freezer paper can be removed while pinning rows together or after they've been sewn together. Add corner triangles and press.

Pieced Border

On the wrong side of fabrics G, H and K border strips, draw a hatch mark 4^1/2" from the end. Simply place 2 rectangles at right angles to each other matching the top edge and mark as illustrated in Figure 19.

Figure 19

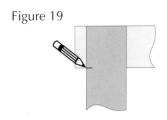

Figure 18

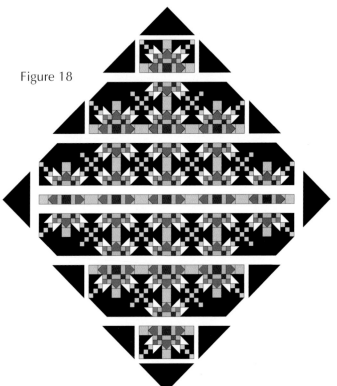

Draw a diagonal line from the outer corner to this mark as illustrated in Figure 20 *(see Shortcuts).*

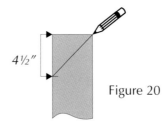

4½"

Figure 20

To make diagonal seams, layer rectangles right sides together as illustrated in Figure 21. Sew on the pencil line. Press seam allowance towards darker fabric and then trim to measure ¼".

Figure 21

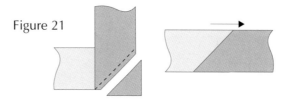

Using diagonal seams, sew border strips together as illustrated in Figure 22. ***Pay particular attention to the direction of the diagonal seams.***

Figure 22

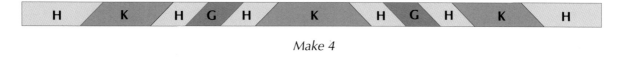

| H | K | H | G | H | K | H | G | H | K | H |

Make 4

Measure the length of your quilt *(through the center of the quilt)* and trim 2 pieced border units to that measurement. Sew to each side of the quilt and press seam towards outer edge. Apply borders to top and bottom using the same technique.

HINT: *To trim pieced borders so they are even on both ends, fold border units in half, wrong sides together. Starting at the fold, measure HALF of the quilt length (or width) measurement and trim off excess fabric.*

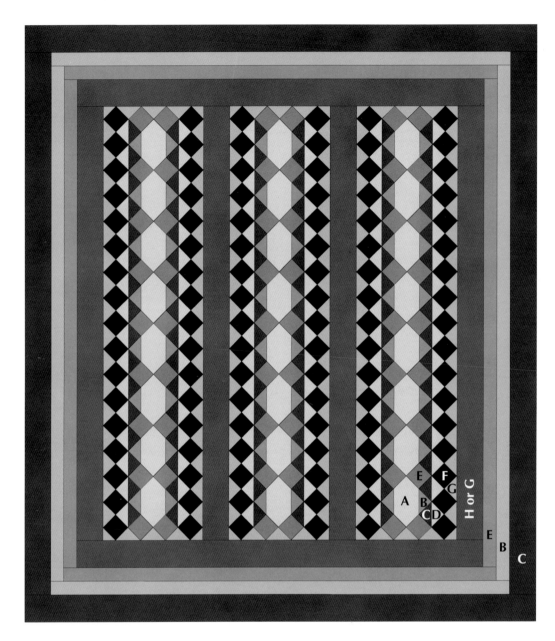

Fishing Rock Lodge *approximate size 75" x 86"*
Remember Aruba *approximate size 67" x 77"*

Fabric Requirements: *photos on pages 34, 37, 55, 56*

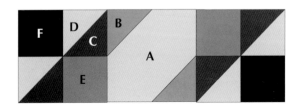

	Fishing Rock Lodge	Remember Aruba
Fabric A	7/8	2 1/8 yard
Fabric B	1 1/8	1/2
Fabric C	1 3/4	3/4
Fabric D	3/4	3/4
Fabric E	1 1/8	5/8
Fabric F	7/8	7/8
Fabric G	3/4	2
Fabric H	1 1/2	—
Binding	3/4	3/4

NOTE: *These cutting instructions are based on having 40" of usable fabric width. If your fabric is even slightly wider, you may have strips left over.*

Cutting Instructions for Fishing Rock Lodge

Fabric A

4 strips	5¹/2" wide	Cut into (24) 5¹/2" squares

Fabric B

4 strips	3" wide	Cut into (48) 3" squares
Border		
7 strips	2¹/2" wide	

Fabric C

5 strips	3³/8" wide	Cut into (48) 3³/8" squares
Border		
8 strips	4¹/2" wide	

Fabric D

5 strips	3³/8" wide	Cut into (48) 3³/8" squares

Fabric E

5 strips	3" wide	Cut into (54) 3" squares
Border		
7 strips	2¹/2" wide	

Fabric F

8 strips	3" wide	Cut into (102) 3" squares

Fabric G

4 strips	4⁷/8" wide	Cut into (29) 4⁷/8" squares cut in half diagonally twice – *setting triangles*
scraps		(6) 2³/4" squares cut in half diagonally once – *corne triangles*

Fabric H

9 strips	4¹/2" wide – *sashing*	

Binding *Fishing Rock Lodge or Remember Aruba*

8 strips	2¹/2" wide	

Cutting Instructions for Remember Aruba

Fabric A

4 strips	5¹/2" wide	Cut into (24) 5¹/2" squares
Border		
7 strips	6" wide	

Do NOT cut these strips if you plan on making half square triangles by drawing a grid or using products such as Triangle Paper™ or Triangles on a Roll™

Cutting Instructions
Remember Aruba

Fabric B

4 strips	3" wide	Cut into (48) 3" squares

Fabric C

◤ 5 strips	3³/₈" wide	Cut into (48) 3³/₈" squares

Fabric D

◤ 5 strips	3³/₈" wide	Cut into (48) 3³/₈" squares

Fabric E

5 strips	3" wide	Cut into (54) 3" squares

Fabric F

8 strips	3" wide	Cut into (102) 3" squares

Fabric G

4 strips	4⁷/₈" wide	Cut into (29) 4⁷/₈" squares cut in half diagonally twice – *setting triangles*
scraps		(6) 2³/₄" squares cut in half diagonally once – *corner triangles*
9 strips	4¹/₂" wide – *sashing*	

Sewing Instructions

Using a sharp pencil, draw a diagonal line on the wrong side of fabric B 3" squares *(see Shortcuts)*.

Figure 1

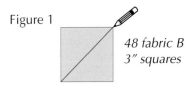

48 fabric B 3" squares

With right sides together place a fabric B 3"square on top of a fabric A 5¹/₂"square as illustrated in Figure 2. Sew on the pencil line. Press seam allowance towards outer edge and trim to measure ¹/₄".

Figure 2

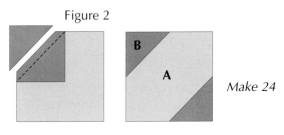

Make 24

Use your favorite technique to make half square triangles or use the following method.

Place fabric C and D 3³/₈"squares right sides together. Cut them in half diagonally. Sew triangles together on the wide edge. Press seam towards darker fabric and trim off dog ears.

Figure 3

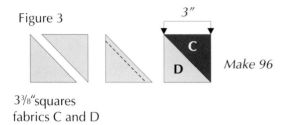

3⅜"squares
fabrics C and D

Make 96

Sew fabric E or F 3" squares onto fabric C/D half square triangle as illustrated in Figure 4. Press seams as arrows indicate.

IMPORTANT NOTE: *Make sure the orientation of your half square triangles match the illustrations.*

Figure 4

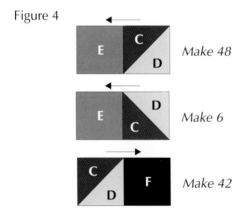

Make 48

Make 6

Make 42

Arrange these half square triangle units as illustrated in Figure 5 and sew them together. Press seam as arrow indicates.

Figure 5

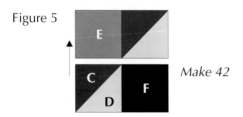

Make 42

Sew 2 fabric G triangles onto fabric F 3" square as illustrated in Figure 6. Press seams as arrows indicate being careful not to stretch the bias edge of the triangles.

Figure 6

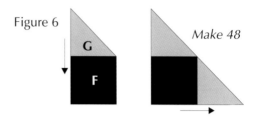

Make 48

Refer to Figure 7 and sew 1 fabric G triangle to fabric F 3" square and fabric C/D/E unit as illustrated.

Figure 7

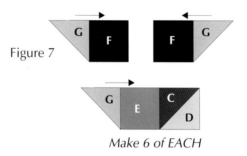

Make 6 of EACH

Sew units together as illustrated in Figure 8. Press seams as arrows indicate.

Figure 8

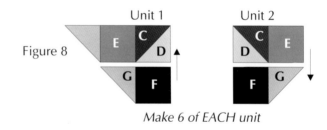

Unit 1   Unit 2

Make 6 of EACH unit

Add fabric F/G triangle to Unit 1 as illustrated in Figure 9. Press seam as arrow indicates.

Unit 1

Figure 9

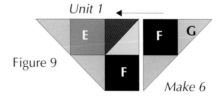

Make 6

Sew pieces together as illustrated in Figure 10. Press seams as arrows indicate handling bias edges carefully. Add fabric G corner triangles as indicated in the illustration.

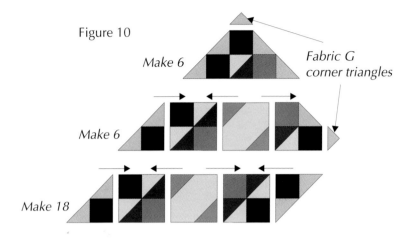

Figure 10

Make 6

Fabric G corner triangles

Make 6

Make 18

DESIGNER TIP: *When matching diagonal seams to straight seams, mark the seam intersecting point on the diagonal seam by drawing a hatch mark $^1/4"$ from the raw edge as illustrated.*

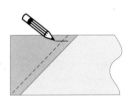

When sewing pieces together, use this hatch mark to align intersecting seams. Place pieces right sides together and match intersecting seam points by pushing a pin straight through the intersection of the diagonal seam and hatch mark and then through the seam of the other unit. Leaving this pin straight, use other pins to secure pieces together by pinning to the right and left of the alignment pin. Remove alignment pin and sew pieces together.

Sew units together to make a row. Make sure the orientation of your pieces match the illustration. Refer to Figure 11. Make 3 rows.

Figure 11

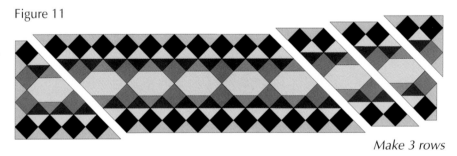

Make 3 rows

Measure the length of the row sections *(through the center)* and make 4 fabric G or H $4^1/2"$ sashing strips to that measurement. Sew a sashing strip onto ONE side of 2 row sections. Press seams towards sashing.

Sew 2 sashing strips onto each side of remaining row section. Press seams as arrows indicate. Using a ruler and a sharp pencil, mark hatch marks *(to match points)* on the raw edges of this center row. Refer to Figure 12. Sew rows together matching these hatch marks with the block points and press.

Figure 12

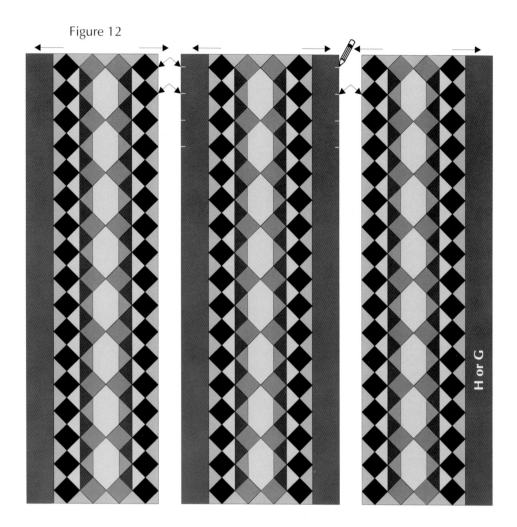

Measure width of quilt *(through the center)* and make 2 fabric G or H 4$^{1}/2$" strips to that measurement. Apply to top and bottom of the quilt and press to outer edge.

General Border Sewing Instructions
Measure the length of your quilt *(through the center of the quilt)* and piece 2 border strips to that measurement. Sew to each side of the quilt and press seam towards outer edge. Apply borders to top and bottom using the same technique.

Remember Aruba Border: Following the general border sewing instructions, apply fabric A (6") border strips.

Fishing Rock Lodge Border: Following the general border sewing instructions, apply fabric E (2$^{1}/2$") inner border strips. Repeat steps to apply fabric B (2$^{1}/2$") border strips. Repeat again for fabric C (4$^{1}/2$") outer border.

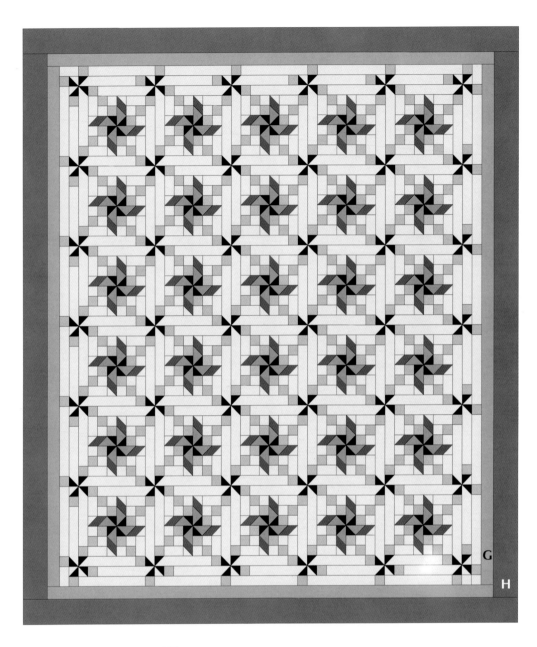

Sweet Dreams *approximate size 84" x 98"*
Calypso *approximate size 87" x 104"*

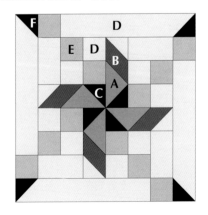

Fabric Requirements: *photos on pages 30, 39, 51, 52*

	Calypso	Sweet Dreams
Fabric A	$^7/_8$	$^7/_8$ yard
Fabric B	$^7/_8$	$^7/_8$
Fabric C	$^1/_2$	$^1/_2$
Fabric D	5	5
Fabric E	$1\,^1/_2$	$3\,^1/_4$
Fabric F	$^7/_8$	$^7/_8$
Fabric G	$1\,^1/_8$	—
Fabric H	$1\,^3/_4$	—
Binding	$^7/_8$	$^7/_8$

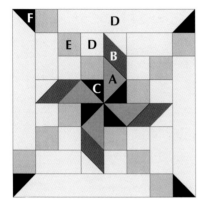

NOTE: *These cutting instructions are based on having 40" of usable fabric width. If your fabric is even slightly wider, you may have strips left over.*

Cutting Instructions for Calypso • Sweet Dreams

Fabric A

5 strips	$4^1/2$" wide	Cut into (80) $4^1/2$" x $2^1/2$" rectangles

OR if you are using stripes *(Sweet Dreams)*

10 strips	$2^1/2$" wide	Cut into (80) $4^1/2$" x $2^1/2$" rectangles

---

Fabric B

5 strips	$4^1/2$" wide	Cut into (80) $4^1/2$" x $2^1/2$" rectangles

---

Fabric C

5 strips	$2^1/2$" wide	Cut into (80) $2^1/2$" squares

Fabric D

43 strips	$2^1/2$" wide	Cut into (98) $12^1/2$" x $2^1/2$" rectangles *and* (18) $14^1/2$" x $2^1/2$" rectangles *and* (80) $2^1/2$" squares
10 strips	$2^1/2$" wide	leave whole
6 strips	$4^1/2$" wide	Cut into (84) $4^1/2$" x $2^1/2$" rectangles
◥ 1 strip	$2^7/8$" wide	Cut into (11) $2^7/8$" squares

Fabric E

18 strips	$2^1/2$" wide	Cut into (120) $2^1/2$" squares and leave 10 strips whole

. . . .

Cut ONLY for Sweet Dreams border

10 strips	6" wide

Fabric F

7 strips	$2^1/2$" wide	Cut into (98) $2^1/2$" squares
◥ 1 strip	$2^7/8$" wide	Cut into (11) $2^7/8$" squares

Fabric G *Cut ONLY for Calypso border*

9 strips	3" wide

Fabric H *Cut ONLY for Calypso border*

10 strips	$5^1/2$" wide

Binding

10 strips	$2^1/2$" wide

◥ *Do NOT cut these strips if you plan on making half square triangles by drawing a grid or using products such as Triangle Paper™ or Triangles on a Roll™*

Sewing Instructions

On the wrong side of fabric B 2^1/$_2$" x 4^1/$_2$" rectangles, draw a hatch mark 2^1/$_2$" from the top. Simply place 2 rectangles at right angles to each other matching the top edge and mark as illustrated in Figure 1.

Figure 1

80 fabric B
2½" x 4½" rectangles

Draw a diagonal line from the outer corner to this mark as illustrated in Figure 2 *(see Shortcuts)*.

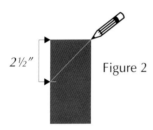

2½"   Figure 2

Layer fabric A and B 2^1/$_2$" x 4^1/$_2$" rectangles right sides together as illustrated in Figure 3. Sew on the pencil line. Press seam allowance as arrow indicates and then trim to measure ^{1}/$_4$".

Figure 3

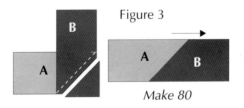

Make 80

Using a sharp pencil, draw a diagonal line on the wrong side of fabric C and D 2^1/$_2$" squares *(see Shortcuts)*.

Figure 4

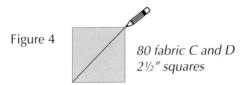

80 fabric C and D
2½" squares

With right sides together, position fabric C 2^1/$_2$" square on the pieced section as illustrated in Figure 5. Stitch on the pencil line. Press seam allowance towards outer edge and then trim to measure ^{1}/$_4$".

Figure 5

Make 80

Repeat these steps, this time using a fabric D 2^1/$_2$" square. Place as illustrated in Figure 6.

Figure 6

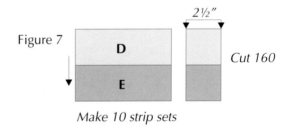

Make 80

Sew fabric D and E 2^1/$_2$" strips together lengthwise. Press seam towards darker fabric. Cutting across the pieced strips, cut into 2^1/$_2$" sections.

Figure 7

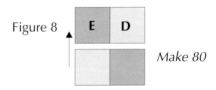

2½"

Cut 160

Make 10 strip sets

Make a 4-patch checkerboard by sewing 2 sections together as illustrated.

Figure 8

Make 80

HINT: *To achieve a nicely joined seam intersection, nestle intersecting seams together before sewing. Do NOT place a pin at the intersecting point.*

Sew fabric D 2¹/₂" x 4¹/₂" rectangle onto the 4-patch as illustrated in Figure 9. Press seam as arrow indicates.

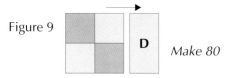

Figure 9   **D**   *Make 80*

NOTE: *Be sure to match the orientation of your 4-patch to the illustrations.*

Sew the pieced sections together as illustrated in Figure 10. Press seam as arrow indicates.

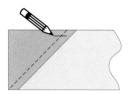

Figure 10   *Make 80*

DESIGNER TIP: *When matching diagonal seams to straight seams, mark the seam intersecting point on the diagonal seam by drawing a hatch mark ¹/₄" from the raw edge as illustrated.*

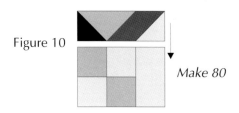

When sewing pieces together, use this hatch mark to align intersecting seams. Place pieces right sides together and match intersecting seam points by pushing a pin straight through the intersection of the diagonal seam and hatch mark and then through the seam of the other unit. Leaving this pin straight, use other pins to secure pieces together by pinning to the right and left of the alignment pin. Remove alignment pin and sew pieces together.

Sew units together to make block as illustrated in Figure 11. Undo several stitches in the seam allowance of the pinwheel center and press seams as arrows indicate.

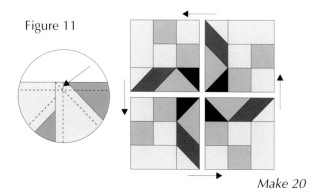

Figure 11   *Make 20*

Sew fabric E 2¹/₂" square onto end of fabric D 12¹/₂" x 2¹/₂" and 14¹/₂" x 2¹/₂" rectangles. Press seams as arrows indicate. Refer to Figure 12.

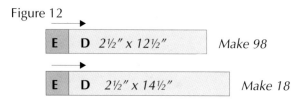

Figure 12

E   **D**   *2½" x 12½"*   *Make 98*

E   **D**   *2½" x 14½"*   *Make 18*

Using a sharp pencil, draw a diagonal line on the wrong side of fabric F 2¹/₂" squares *(see Shortcuts)*.

Figure 13   *98 fabric F 2½" squares*

With right sides together, position a fabric F 2¹/₂" square on the corner of fabric D/E units as illustrated in Figure 14. Stitch on the pencil line. Press seam towards outer edge and then trim seam allowance to ¹/₄".

Mark ¹/₄" seam allowance across diagonal seams *(see Designer Tip)*.

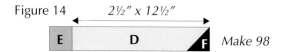

Figure 14   *2½" x 12½"*

E   **D**   **F**   *Make 98*

With right sides together, sew ²/₃ of unit D/E/F onto block as illustrated in Figure 15.
Fingerpress this partial seam as arrow indicates.

Figure 15

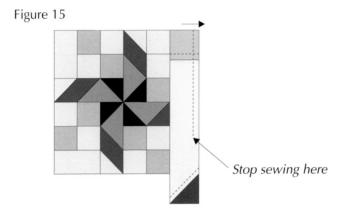

Stop sewing here

Add next 3 sections in the order illustrated in Figure 16. Carefully press each seam as you go
along. The last seam will complete the partial seam you started with.

Figure 16

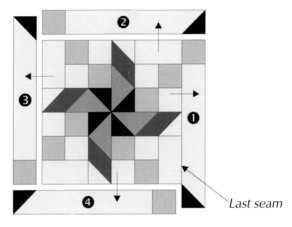

Last seam

HINT: *In the event some **slight** easing is required, place the section
needing to be eased next to the feed dogs when sewing units
together. Refer to Designer Tip to align the diagonal seam of the
pinwheel to the straight seam of the chain.*

Use your favorite technique to make half square triangles or use the following method.

Place fabric D and F 2⁷/₈" squares right sides together. Cut them in half diagonally. Sew
triangles together on the wide edge. Press seam towards darker fabric and trim off dog ears.

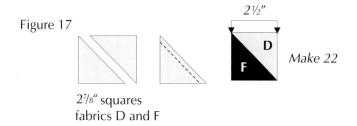

Figure 17

2½"

D

F

Make 22

2⅞" squares
fabrics D and F

Sew half square triangle onto end of fabric D/F/E unit as illustrated in Figure 18. Press seam as arrow indicates.

Sew units together as illustrated in Figure 18. *Only press the seams indicated by arrows. Leave other seams to be pressed later.*

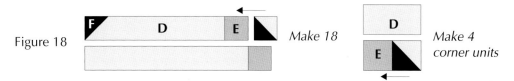

Figure 18

F D E

Make 18

D

E

Make 4
corner units

Refer to Figure 19 and press unit seams as indicated. Sew units into rows. Press seams as arrows indicate.

Figure 19

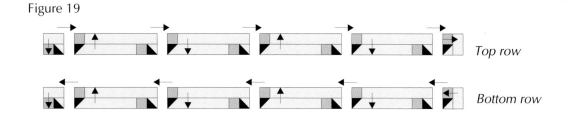

Top row

Bottom row

Refer to Figure 20 and sew blocks and remaining D/E/F units into rows as illustrated. Press seams as arrows indicate. Sew rows together and press.

General Border Application Instructions

Measure the length of your quilt *(through the center of the quilt)* and piece 2 border strips to that measurement. Sew to each side of the quilt and press seam towards outer edge. Apply borders to top and bottom using the same technique.

Sweet Dreams Border: Following the general border sewing instructions, apply fabric E (6") border strips.

Calypso Border: Following the general border sewing instructions, apply fabric G (3") inner border strips. Repeat steps to apply fabric H (5½") outer border strips.

Figure 20

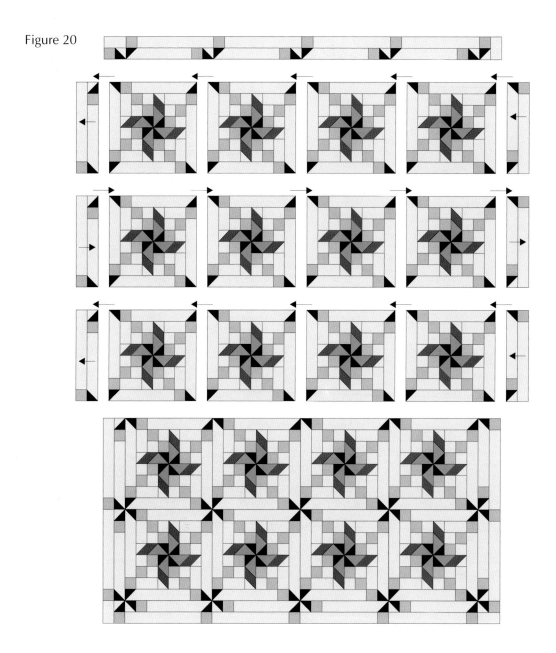

NOTE: *Refer to Designer Tip when aligning the diagonal seams of the pinwheels and the straight seams of the chain.*

Indian Summer *approximate size 65" x 78"*

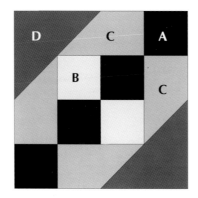

Fabric Requirements: *photos on pages 24, 54*

Fabric A	1¹/₈ yards
Fabric B	³/₄
Fabric C	***6 assorted fabrics***
	¹/₂ of 5 fabrics
	²/₃ of 1 fabric
Fabric D	3³/₈*
Fabric E	1

*Includes binding

NOTE: These cutting instructions are based on having 40" of usable fabric width. If your fabric is even slightly wider, you may have strips left over.

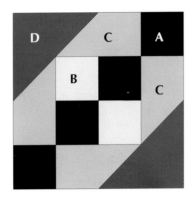

Cutting Instructions for Indian Summer

Fabric A

13 strips	$2^1/2$" wide

Fabric B

7 strips	$2^1/2$" wide

Fabric C *6 fabrics (cut 1 strip from 5 fabrics and 2 strips from 6th fabric)*
7 strips $6^1/2$" wide — since you will only use $6^1/2$ of these strips, cut 1 strip in half and from the leftover half cut:

(8) $2^1/2$" x $4^1/2$" rectangles

6 strips	$4^1/2$" wide	Cut into (92) $2^1/2$" x $4^1/2$" rectangles
	scraps	(8) $4^1/2$" squares *(assorted colors)*

Fabric D

14 strips	$4^1/2$" wide	Cut into (110) $4^1/2$" squares
Border		
7 strips	$4^1/2$" wide	
Binding		
7 strips	$2^1/2$" wide	

Fabric E *Setting triangles*

2 strips	$12^3/4$" wide	Cut into (5) $12^3/4$" squares cut in half diagonally twice — *setting triangles*
	scraps	(2) $6^3/4$" squares cut in half diagonally once — *corner triangles*

Sewing Instructions

With right sides together, sew fabric A and B $2^1/2$" strips and fabric C $6^1/2$" strips together lengthwise as illustrated in Figure 1. Press seams as arrows indicate. Cutting across the pieced strip sets, cut into $2^1/2$" sections. Cut fabric A/C units in matching sets of 2.

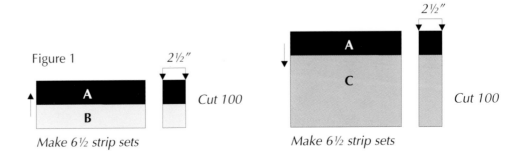

Figure 1

Make 6½ strip sets

Cut 100

Make 6½ strip sets

Cut 100

Vivaldi: Figure 13

Vivaldi: Figure 12

A | Unit 1 | Unit 1 | Unit 1 | Unit 1 | B

Make 2 rows

Unit 2 | | | | | Unit 2

Make 4 rows

D | F | | | |

Make 5 rows

IMPORTANT NOTE: *The differences between the block layout illustrations of Vivaldi and Jasmine are the orientation of fabrics A and B within the blocks as well as the location of Units 1 and Units 2. Take a moment to familiarize yourself with these differences. Although subtle, each layout creates it's own unique overall effect. See color photographs on pages 59 and 60.*

Jasmine: Figure 13

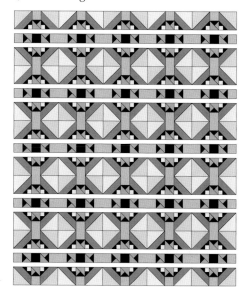

Jasmine: Figure 12

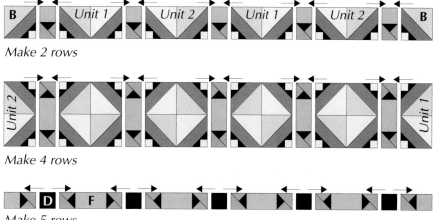

B | Unit 1 | Unit 2 | Unit 1 | Unit 2 | B

Make 2 rows

Unit 2 | | | | | Unit 1

Make 4 rows

D | F | | | |

Make 5 rows

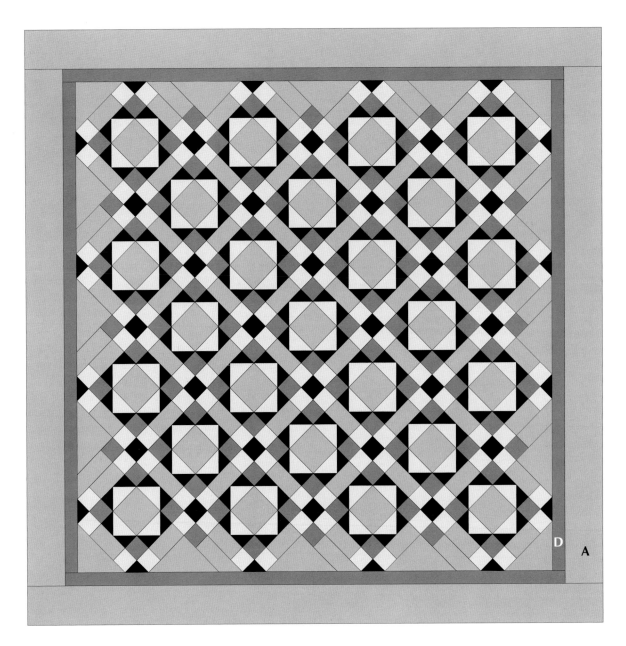

Victoria Garden • Hot Stuff *approximate size 68" x 68"*

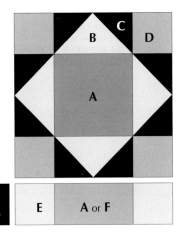

Fabric Requirements: *photos on pages 14, 40, 61, 62*

	Victoria Garden	Hot Stuff
Fabric A	$3^3/8$*	$2^7/8$* yards
Fabric B	$1^1/8$	$1^1/8$
Fabric C	$1^3/8$	$1^1/8$
Fabric D	$1^1/4$	$1^1/4$
Fabric E	$^3/4$	$^3/4$
Fabric F	—	$^3/4$
Fabric G	—	$^3/8$

*Includes Binding

NOTE: *These cutting instructions are based on having 40" of usable fabric width. If your fabric is even slightly wider, you may have strips left over.*

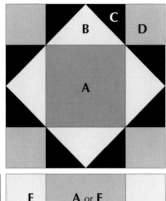

Cutting Instructions for Hot Stuff • Victoria Garden

Fabric A
3 strips	4¹/₂" wide	Cut into (25) 4¹/₂" squares
1 strip	9³/₄" wide	Cut into (3) 9³/₄" squares cut in half diagonally twice — *setting triangles*
	scraps	(2) 6¹/₂" squares cut in half diagonally once —*corner triangles*
1 strip	7¹/₂" wide	
Outer Border		
8 strips	5" wide	
Binding		
8 strips	2¹/₂" wide	

· ·

Cut ONLY for **Victoria Garden**
4 strips	4¹/₂" wide	

Fabric B
7 strips	4¹/₂" wide	Cut into (100) 2¹/₂" x 4¹/₂" rectangles

OR if you are using stripes or directional fabric
13 strips	2¹/₂" wide	Cut into (100) 2¹/₂" x 4¹/₂" rectangles

Fabric C
13 strips	2¹/₂" wide	Cut into (200) 2¹/₂" squares

· ·

Cut ONLY for **Victoria Garden**
2 strips	2¹/₂" wide	Cut into (24) 2¹/₂" squares
1 strip	4¹/₄" wide	Cut into (4) 4¹/₄" squares cut in half diagonally twice

Fabric D
8 strips	2¹/₂" wide	Cut into (100) 2¹/₂" squares – *leave 1 strip whole*
Inner Border		
7 strips	1³/₄" wide	

Fabric E
8 strips	2¹/₂" wide	

Cutting Instructions
Continued

Fabric F *cut ONLY for* **Hot Stuff**

*Use these cutting instructions if your fabric is **NOT** directional, if you are using directional or striped fabric, refer to the special cutting instructions below.*

4 strips   4¹/2" wide

Designer Tip 🖝 **Special Cutting Instructions for Directional or Striped Fabric**

Cut 1 section 21" long from your yardage. Open fabric so you are working with a single layer. Trim off selvage by lining up your ruler evenly against one of the stripes (or a row of motifs). Cut the indicated strips from this edge, resquaring your fabric often.

8 strips   4¹/2" wide *(these strips will be 21" long)*

Fabric G *cut ONLY for* **Hot Stuff**

2 strips	2¹/2" wide	Cut into (24) 2¹/2" squares
1 strip	4¹/4" wide	Cut into (4) 4¹/4" squares cut in half diagonally twice

---

Sewing Instructions

Draw a diagonal line on the wrong side of fabric C 2¹/2" squares *(see Shortcuts)*.

Figure 1

200 fabric C 2½" squares

With right sides together, position a fabric C 2¹/2" square on the corner of a fabric B 2¹/2" x 4¹/2" rectangle. Stitch on the pencil line.

Press seam towards outer edge and then trim seam allowance to measure ¹/4". Repeat these steps for the other corner. Refer to Figure 2.

Figure 2

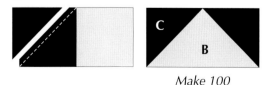

Make 100

Sew a fabric D 2¹/2" square onto each end of this unit. Press seams as arrows indicate.

Figure 3

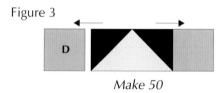

Make 50

Sew remaining units to sides of fabric A 4¹/2" square as illustrated in Figure 4. Press seams as arrows indicate.

Figure 4

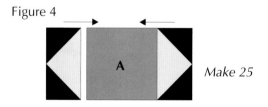

Make 25

Sew sections together as illustrated in Figure 5. Press seams as arrows indicate.

Figure 5

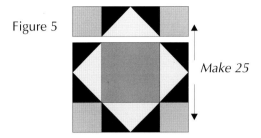

Make 25

Sew fabric E 2¹/2" strips and fabric A or F 4¹/2" strips together lengthwise as illustrated in Figure 6. Press seams as arrows indicate.

Sew a fabric D 2¹/2" strip and fabric A 7¹/2" strip together lengthwise as illustrated in Figure 6. Press seams as arrows indicate. Cut pieced strip sets into 2¹/2" sections.

Figure 6

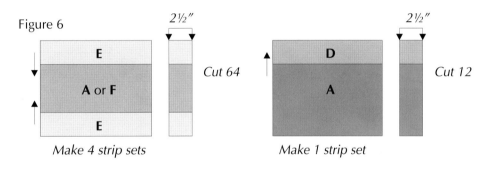

Make 4 strip sets   *Make 1 strip set*

NOTE: *If you are using a directional fabric and have cut short strips (21" long), count each short strip as a half strip.*

Sew fabric A/D unit onto side of setting triangle as illustrated in Figure 7. Using a ruler and rotary cutter, trim off excess fabric so triangle edge is even.

Figure 7

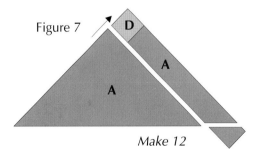

Make 12

Refer to Figure 8 and arrange blocks, setting/corner triangles, fabric E/F units and fabric G or C 2¹/2" squares and triangles as illustrated. Sew pieces into diagonal rows. Press seams as arrows indicate. Sew rows together and press. If necessary, trim so quilt edge is even.

Border

Measure the quilt *(through the center of your quilt)* and piece 2 inner border strips (1³/₄") to that measurement. Sew to each side of the quilt and press towards outer edge.

Apply inner border to top and bottom of the quilt using the same technique. Repeat these steps, this time using the outer border (5") fabric strips.

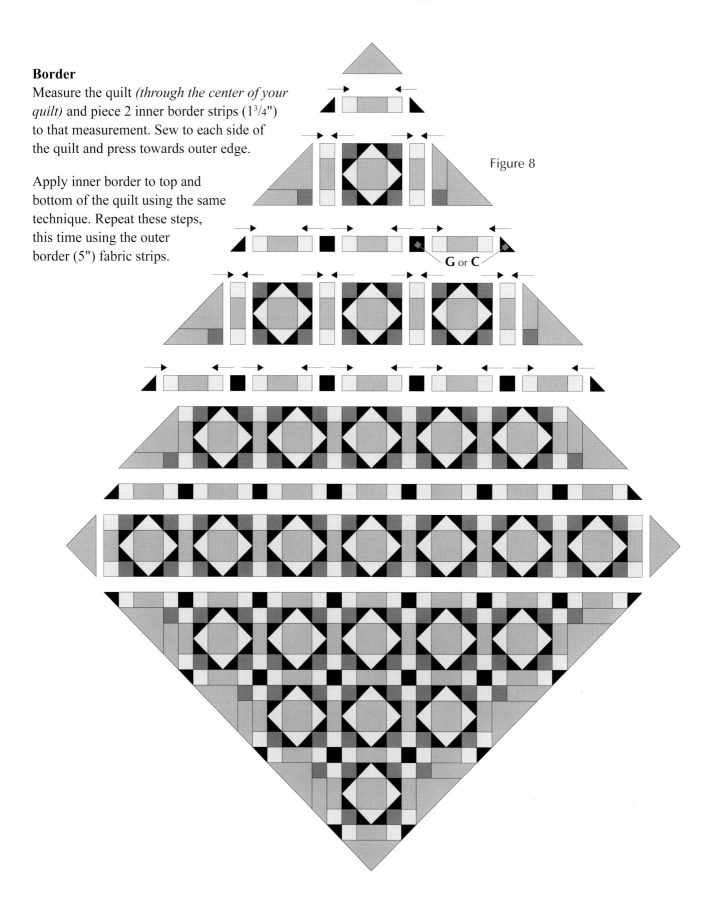

Figure 8

G or **C**

An Amish Hound • Happy Days *approximate size 52" x 64"*

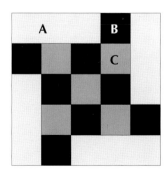

Fabric Requirements: *photos on pages 8, 26, 47, 48*

	Happy Days*	An Amish Hound*
Fabric A	$2^1/4$	$2^1/4$ yards
Fabric B	$1^7/8$	10 fat quarters
Fabric C	2	$2^1/4$

*Includes border and binding

Cutting Instructions for Happy Days

NOTE: *These cutting instructions are based on having 40" of usable fabric width. If your fabric is even slightly wider, you may have strips left over.*

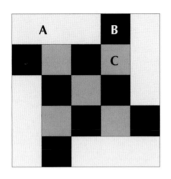

Fabric A
8 strips	$6^1/2$" wide
7 strips	$2^1/2$" wide

Fabric B
16 strips	$2^1/2$" wide
Border	
7 strips	$2^1/2$" wide

Fabric C
10 strips	$2^1/2$" wide
Border	
7 strips	$2^1/2$" wide
Binding	
7 strips	$2^1/2$" wide

Cutting Instructions for An Amish Hound

IMPORTANT NOTE: *When making these blocks scrappy, it is easier to sew the individual squares and rectangles together rather than strip piecing them. Refer to the Special Sewing Instructions for An Amish Hound as your 1st step, after that follow the general sewing instructions.*

Fabric A
8 strips	$6^1/2$" wide	Cut into (120) $2^1/2$" x $6^1/2$" rectangles
7 strips	$2^1/2$" wide	

Fabric B *assortment of 10 fat quarters (cut on the wide edge of fat quarter)*
38 strips*	$2^1/2$" wide	Cut into (302) $2^1/2$" squares
		if you are cutting full strips from yardage, cut only 19 strips

Fabric C
14 strips*	$2^1/2$" wide	Cut into (212) $2^1/2$" squares
4 strips**	$4^1/2$" wide	Cut into (64) $2^1/2$" x $4^1/2$" rectangles
Binding		
7 strips	$2^1/2$" wide	

*Includes pieces for pieced border
**For pieced border only

If you are making An Amish Hound ...

Note the following matching units you will need to complete 1 block when you are making your quilt scrappy.

Figure 1A

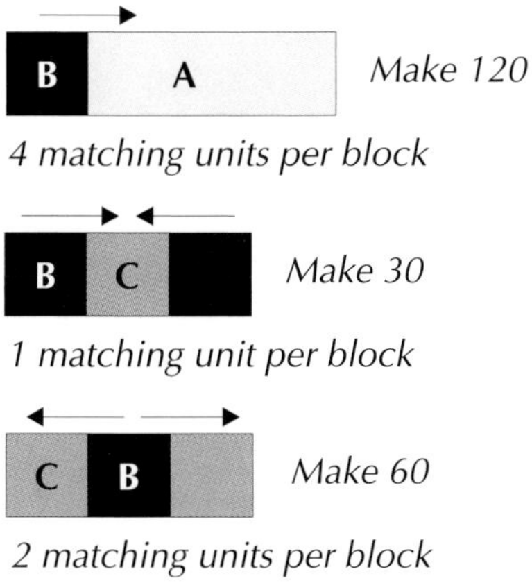

Make 120

4 matching units per block

Make 30

1 matching unit per block

Make 60

2 matching units per block

Sew fabric B and C 2¹/₂" squares and fabric A 2¹/₂" x 6¹/₂" rectangles together as illustrated. Press seams as arrows indicate.

IMPORTANT NOTE: *Be sure to press seams as arrows indicate even though it goes against convention.*

Once these units illustrated in Figure 1A are made, refer to Figure 2 to continue making your quilt.

If you are making Happy Days ...

Refer to Figure 1B and sew indicated fabric B and C 2¹/₂" and fabric A 6¹/₂" strips together lengthwise. Press seams as arrows indicate. Cutting across the pieced strip sets, cut into 2¹/₂" sections.

Figure 1B

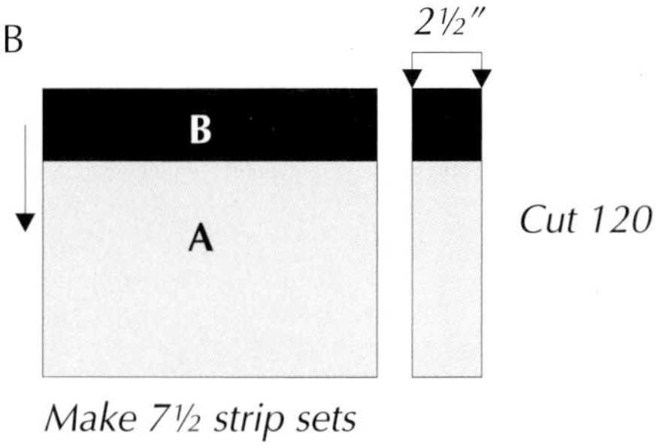

2¹/₂"

Cut 120

Make 7½ strip sets

Figure 1B *continued*

2¹/₂"

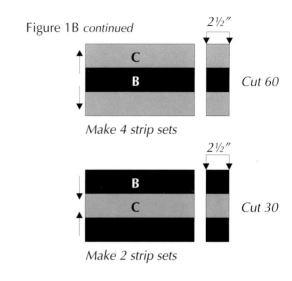

Cut 60

Make 4 strip sets

2¹/₂"

Cut 30

Make 2 strip sets

Make a 9-patch checkerboard by sewing B/C units together as illustrated in Figure 2. Press seams as arrows indicate.

Figure 2

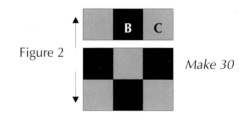

Make 30

NOTE: *Be sure to match orientation of your pieces to the illustrations.*

With right sides together, sew ²/₃ of fabric A/B unit onto checkerboard as illustrated. Refer to Figure 3.

Stop here

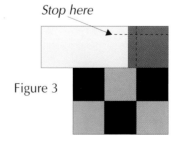

Figure 3

Add the next 3 A/B sections in the order illustrated in Figure 4. Carefully press each seam as you go along. The last seam will complete the partial seam you started with.

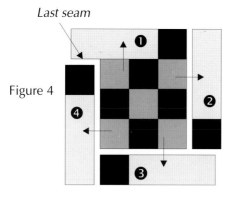

Last seam

Figure 4

Sew 5 blocks together to form a row. Press seams as arrows indicate in Figure 5.

Figure 5

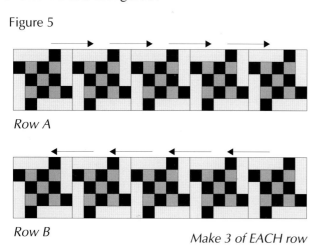

Row A

Row B

Make 3 of EACH row

Sew rows together alternating rows A and B so seams butt together and press.

Measure the length of your quilt *(through the center of the quilt)* and piece 2 fabric A strips (2¹/2") to that measurement. Sew to sides of the quilt and press seams towards outer edge. Apply fabric A strips to top and bottom of the quilt using the same technique.

Happy Days Border
Measure the length of your quilt *(through the center of the quilt)* and piece 2 fabric C strips 2¹/2" to that measurement. Sew to sides of the quilt and press seams towards outer edge. Apply fabric C strips to top and bottom of the quilt using the same technique.

Repeat these steps, this time using fabric B 2¹/2" strips.

An Amish Hound Pieced Border
Sew fabric B and C 2¹/2" squares together as illustrated in Figure 6. Press seam as arrow indicates.

Figure 6

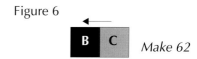

Make 62

Refer to Figure 7 and sew B/C units and fabric C 2¹/2" x 4¹/2" rectangles together to make Border Units #1 – #4 as illustrated. Press seams towards fabric C rectangles as arrows indicate.

Starting with Border Unit #1, sew border onto top of quilt as illustrated. Leave 12" of the border unattached. Press seam towards inner border as arrow indicates.

Next, sew Border Unit #2 onto right side of quilt as illustrated in Figure 7. Press seam as arrow indicates. Repeat these steps to apply Border Units #3 and #4. Finish off by sewing the 12" of Border Unit #1 onto quilt and press.

Figure 7

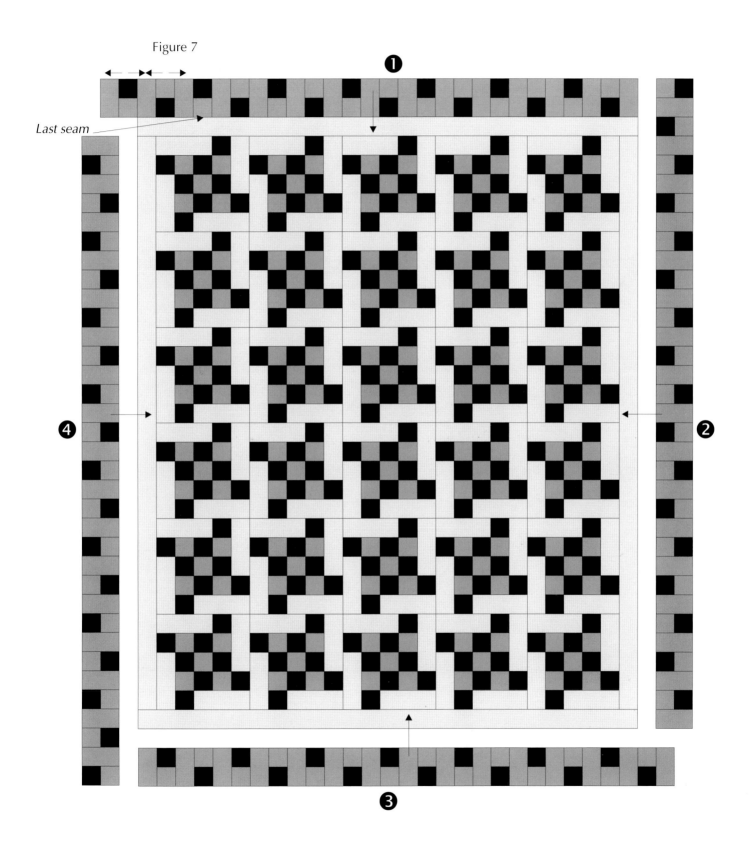

Last seam

ABOUT THE AUTHOR

Nicole Chambers is a quilt designer and quilting instructor known for her unique color sense and stylish quilt designs. Her clear, easy-to-follow instructions have been praised and appreciated by new and experienced quilters alike. In her last book, *The Quilt Maniac's PLAYBOOK: Fuel for the Quilt Imagination*, many quilters learned the secrets of how to work with colors and fabric patterns to achieve the quilts they envision.

It became self evident very early in life that Nicole was born to be a quilter. She started building her stash at the tender age of 6 by charming all of the neighbor ladies into giving up their fabric scraps — much to the chagrin of her mother. Before starting her pattern company, Nicole's Art to Live With in 1994; Nicole used her creative design and writing skills by working for many years as a Communications Specialist for a variety of companies. Although she thoroughly enjoyed this career, when she found herself sneaking quilting books into the office in "plain brown wrappers," it was time to reconsider her career path. It was then that she decided to turn her talents towards the quilting world.

Nicole considers quilting to be a very important avenue of self expression and finds it no accident that so many women and men are such enthusiastic participants. It allows the creative spirit to soar while allowing us to leave a trail of memories behind to remind our loved ones just how dear they are.

She is committed to teaching and encouraging all quilters to honor their unique creativity, always coaxing them to stretch themselves a little with every quilting project. Motivated by the recognition that it can be hard to find time to indulge our passion to quilt as much as we would like to, Nicole drafts her patterns with a keen eye towards quality. She remembers well the precious moments we finally have for ourself at the end of a taxing day, or the frustration we feel when we can't figure out what the next step is and at 2:00 AM find ourself wondering if it would be reasonable to ask the telephone operator if she quilts.

Nicole has won awards for both quilting and photography. She and her son Aaron live on the Oregon Coast.

INDEX

RESOURCES

Patterns and books are available at your local quilt shop or from
Nicole's Art to Live With & Tiger Lily Press
PO Box 740 • Depoe Bay, OR 97341
(541) 764-2778 • www.nicolechambers.com

Other designs by Nicole Chambers

Books:
- The Quilt Maniac's PLAYBOOK: Fuel for the Quilt Imagination
  > ***A Special Note to Quilt Teachers:*** *"The Ultimate Workshop Companion & Teachers Guide for The Quilt Maniac's PLAYBOOK" is now available to shop owners and quilt teachers. It features exclusive workshop sized versions of 9 queen sized quilts and has everything you need to give great workshops including handouts.*

Patterns:
- A Quilt for Betsy Ross
- Dancing in the Moonlight
- Smarter than the Average Bear
- Miss Eva's Garden
- Classroom Sampler
- Wild Roses from Milan
- Spring
- Summer
- Autumn
- Winter
- Apple Pie
- La Fleur

Block of the Month Series:
- Family Treasures
- As Time Goes By

OOQ™ Mystery Series:
- Operation: Weather or Not
- The Rose Blooms at Midnight
- My Fine Feathered Friend
- A Night at the Opera
- The Moon Wore Sneakers

Products that have been mentioned in the book are as follows:

Triangle Paper™
www.quiltime.com

Triangles on a Roll™
www.trianglesonaroll.com